S0-FQY-081

Sifted Gold

SIFTED GOLD

Yvonne M. Wilson

CONCORDIA
Publishing House
St. Louis   London

Concordia Publishing House, St. Louis, Missouri
Concordia Publishing House Ltd., London E. C. 1
Copyright © 1974 Concordia Publishing House
Library of Congress Catalog Card No. 74-4743
ISBN 0-570-03235-0

MANUFACTURED IN THE UNITED STATES OF AMERICA

DEDICATION

To my husband Dan, my son Ted, my daughter Dana Lynn, my son-in-law Dennis; and to Kyle, our grandson, only nine months old then, who tolerated the confusion and remained a happy little fellow. To these I dedicate this book—for their unwavering love, their physical, mental, and spiritual support when their own emotional and physical strength was being overtaxed.

I am also forever indebted to my friends for their love and understanding through my illness and my recovery.

Especially I am indebted to Pat Harrison for her inspiration and constant source of encouragement as well as her hard secretarial work throughout the writing of my manuscript; to Julia C. Davis for her expert correction of sentence structure; and to Anna Louise Anderson for her careful typing of the finished copy. I am also appreciative of Dr. Alfred Rees for reading and checking from the physician's standpoint; and to Rev. George Ross for reading from the viewpoint of the theologian.

Explanations and Permissions

Scripture references not otherwise marked are from the King James Version. The following abbreviations are used for other versions quoted: AB for the Amplified Bible, LB for the Living Bible, NEB for the New English Bible, and RSV for the Revised Standard Version. "Phillips" stands for J. B. Phillips' New Testament in Modern English.

Words in italics sometimes shown in Scripture quotations are for emphasis and are the author's own. The same is true for the italics shown in a quotation from *The Silver Chalice,* by Thomas B. Costain.

Acknowledgements go to the following for granting permission to quote from their books and other publications:

Abingdon Press, for use of "Open My Eyes, That I May See," from the 1966 edition of *The Book of Hymns;* also for permission to quote from *Psychology, Religion, and Healing,* by Leslie D. Weatherhead, 1952;

Beechwood Music Corporation, for use of the song title "Put Your Hand in the Hand";

Concordia Publishing House, for permission to quote from *Good Lord, Where Are You?* by Leslie Brandt, 1967;

Doubleday and Company, Inc., for permission to quote from *The Silver Chalice,* by Thomas B. Costain, 1952;

Fleming H. Revell Company, for letting me quote from *God's Psychiatry,* by Charles L. Allen, 1953, and from *The Miracle of Love,* by Charles L. Allen, 1972;

Harper and Row Publishers, Inc., for use of *Find and Use Your Inner Power,* by Emmet Fox, 1941;

Unity School of Christianity, for permitting me to quote the two poems: "Watchfulness," author unknown, and "Results," by Elizabeth Landewear;

Zondervan Publishing House, for the use of *Make Love Your Aim,* by Eugenia Price, 1967.

Introduction

I'd like you to meet a miracle! You perhaps would not think so just seeing her. But, believe me, she is a miracle. Her name is Yvonne Wilson. Her story is indeed miraculous. You will agree after having read it. She is a rare combination of wit and perception;

of insecurity and quiet confidence;

of doubt and deep faith;

of fear and raw courage.

I first met Yvonne on a hot summer afternoon in Lafayette, Louisiana. She and her family had recently moved to our city from Jackson, Mississippi. After having received the local minister with her customary southern graciousness, she soon made me aware of her skepticism at being transplanted into Acadiana country. The land of Evangeline was a big change from the lovely city she had left. Since I myself had been in southwest Louisiana for only a short time, I understood her feelings. However, the friendliness of these people soon captivates everyone.

From our first meeting until the dramatic moment which spelled tragedy and victory for Yvonne, we

9

established a splendid rapport. However, this warm relationship was limited to a minister-parishioner acquaintance until I was called shortly after eight o'clock one very warm morning in May. The voice on the other end of the line said, "Reverend Ross, you had better come to Yvonne Wilson's home right away! We have discovered Yvonne on her bedroom floor dead! It looks like suicide!"

That long trip from her home to the emergency room at Lafayette General Hospital and those moments — which seemed like hours — in the ambulance enabled our relationship to emerge as a friendship in the deepest sense, because we understood we were in the presence of life, of death, and of the Holy Spirit.

I'd like you to meet a miracle! Yvonne, tell your story. Believe that God will give His grace as you witness to His work in your life. Then gold dust will fall into our lives.

REV. GEORGE W. ROSS
New Orleans, Louisiana

Sifted Gold

The original title of this book was to have been *Hope Beyond Tragedy.* This was how I felt in those early months of my illness when I was grasping for security and *Hope;* and certainly all will agree that my immediate existence was that of *Tragedy.*

However, in the first chapters of this book I related actual experiences of mine involving my illness, miracles that transpired, my relation with and beliefs about the Holy Spirit, my battle with doubts and fears, and so on. As I became further involved in the writing of later chapters, I did much questioning and searching. I tried to transmit my own sincere beliefs. In so doing, I found it necessary, while writing or shortly thereafter, to change my thinking and be more definite in my feelings. I have contributed this to be a *sifting* of the parts that make up the spirit, the mind, the heart, the soul. It has been an humbling experience, proving God's concern for my happiness. This sifting removed the *tragedy,* made the *hope* emphatic, and thus destroyed the original title.

It is through these *siftings* that one hopes to have gathered a sprinkling of *gold* dust.

Preface

On May 13, 1971, no one would have surmised that 14 months later I would be forcing a pen between my thumb and forefinger and scribbling notes for this book. Nor would it seem possible that today I am learning to walk again with the aid of a walker. In fact, on that Thursday, and for many months thereafter, no one would have given a nickel for my life.

Six days earlier, on the Friday evening preceding this unfathomable day, I had gone to bed feeling exhausted. I was sure this was caused from an overcrowded schedule that week and especially that particular day. But the busy day was over, and after a good night's rest I would be ready for and excited over a trip planned to Florida the next day. I have not made that trip yet.

Shortly after retiring I felt extreme nausea and had every indication of a "bug" or virus. By telephone I reached the doctor on call that evening and he prescribed medication. Soon I began to feel very cold and was plagued with hard chills that did not subside easily with blankets and heating pad. Then followed the aching, a headache, and temperature of 105 degrees.

At this point the doctor suggested aspirin and that if I were no better by the next morning I might check further with him. Eventually the temperature relented and I fell asleep. However, the virus continued to nag me, and the following Monday I was given a different medicine.

Nothing seemed to help the virus, and it was on Wesnesday evening, only two hours before my tragic night began, that because of difficulty in swallowing and sluggish speech I saw Doctor Rees at the hospital. After examining and finding no indications of anything serious, he believed that I was experiencing intoxication from the two different medications given me that week for the virus.

This was not the case, however. Both tragedies and miracles that have affected and changed the course of my life followed, involving and leaving its marks on my family and many friends.

Why am I writing this book? I prayed in those early months that, if it were God's will that I should live, He would use me and my illness as an instrument to glorify His name. It is my hope that readers will find in these pages my witness for Christ; that through my personal experiences others who face such dire circumstances in their lives may gain insight into God's concern for all His children.

It is by faith in God that we are able to withstand that which happens to us. Faith gives us an anchor with which to hold firmly. "That person is secure who draws his strength from God." (Paraphrase on Psalm 146:5, from *Good Lord, Where Are You?*, by Leslie F. Brandt)

Contents

1

Too Confused to Pray

It was shortly before midnight that I awoke abruptly with the earthshaking awareness that something terrifying was happening to me. My mouth and throat seemed to be closing in on me. My tongue and jaws felt thick and swollen, and the tongue seemed to be filling my whole mouth and choking me. My cheeks and neck felt numb. Even my nose seemed three times its normal size.

Propping up in bed, I tried to talk out loud; but there was only a weird sound of mumbling. I worked hard at saying names—names of friends to call on the telephone for help. I even tried saying my own name in order to let the person on the other end of the receiver know who I was; because I knew my voice was not recognizable. My tongue would roll in my mouth, and the only sound I was making was a deep, gravel-like noise that suddenly faded into no sound at all.

In my confusion I did not consider that in an emergency one should simply call the operator and that she could handle things from there. Nevertheless it would not have mattered, because all reasoning or

17

endeavor on my part was in vain. My condition was to become decidedly worse before the night was over.

For a while fear and panic overpowered me. I could not make enough noise for anyone in an adjoining room to hear me pleading for help. But the appalling fact was that there was no one in any other room of the house. In fact, there was not a member of my family within 200 miles; it could just as well have been 2,000.

It was an extremely long night—10 hours, to be exact. It seemed an eternity that found me alone in a nightmarish struggle with a fast-moving paralysis starting with my throat and face and descending to every extremity of my body, leaving me almost lifeless and completely helpless.

Let me say here that the thought of paralysis did not occur to me through this whole night of terrifying events. I was too concerned with what was happening to me to put a label on it. I was to be confronted with the horrible word PARALYZED sometime later.

I had used enough foresight that night to put the telephone on the bed beside me. However, as I said before, all practical reasoning proved to be in vain. At this point I decided to dial my friend who had taken me to see the doctor earlier. Since she was aware of and concerned with my feeling slightly ill, I hoped that she would suspect it was I and understand my predicament.

Still not realizing how much trouble I was in, I took the receiver off the hook only to find that my fingers were absolutely limp and I had no control of them, nor of my hands. My arms were seemingly strong enough, but as I would frantically try time and again to use the telephone, they absolutely would not propel in the direction to which I was aiming. I was losing coordination all over my body and was feeling very weak.

I was also losing the stability of my back and shoulders, and every effort to balance myself seemed futile. By now I was having difficulty holding myself in a sitting position on the bed. I felt real panic but resigned myself to the fact that I must remain calm and make every effort possible to use the telephone to seek help. This time I tried to brace myself in a position to use the telephone without falling, but my limbs would not cooperate with my efforts. They were going in every direction except the way I needed them to go. My left leg went completely out of control and threw me off balance, making me fall in one shocking moment from the bed onto the floor.

In the fall I knocked the receiver off the hook and it dangled from the bed as I lay helpless on my left side. What a feeling of despair! Immediately upon falling I became aware of inability to swallow my saliva, which drained down my cheek as I lay on my side. I didn't know what this meant; certainly I had no idea that my throat was paralyzed. Had I known, I would have been even more desperate, if that were possible. There must be something I could do — but what? Surely, no, it wasn't conceivable that I should be forced to succumb — lying on this floor without a fighting chance!

Perhaps you have lain awake sometimes at night and felt the stillness and quietness of the dark hours when nothing stirred. Alone that night, I have never known such solitude! However, to break this terrible silence, every hour and every half hour there was our old clock striking, keeping me informed of the time.

I counted every strike. I was conscious of the ticktock as the pendulum swung back and forth. That was the only distraction I had from my own fears. Momentarily, as I fell to the floor, this timekeeper struck two, then two-thirty, and three. My only hope was to use that telephone! I was able to pull myself up to a sitting position but somehow lost control of the situation, and one unexpected agonizing jerk of my body pulled me back to the floor. This time I fell on my right side with saliva draining down my right cheek.

Four o'clock, five, six, and seven — I was lying there thinking, trying to convince myself that it is important to remain calm in such a crisis as this. But mostly I was trying to pray. I remember that I was too confused and too weak to pray as hard as I desired or felt necessary. Someone had to be watching over me, because I certainly couldn't do much for myself.

I did convince myself once more that I had enough strength to use the telephone. This was my big mistake. I pulled and tugged to get to a sitting position again and desperately struggled for the telephone. I was so close, with my hands barely touching it, when suddenly my neck melted. My head felt like a ton of weight and pulled me to the floor for the last time. This time I fell on my back, and immediately I knew I was in real trouble. I could not swallow the saliva nor could it drain, although surely part of it was seeping down my throat. I was aware that my lungs were filling with this fluid, which felt like pints of foamy water. I was choking, but I could not cough, nor could I control my predicament in any way. I thought that whatever was happening to me, whatever the problem causing my whole being to play out, I was surely dying from drowning. I was also having a hard time breathing, and I was very tired and weak. By now there was total resignation on my part.

This was my plight for the rest of the morning until I was found in a comatose state at approximately nine-thirty. This was also my first miracle. How else could I have remained alive through so much?

2

Strength Through Weakness

Many people have asked me what it is like to spend such a night as I have described. It is beyond their conception, and understandably so. Almost constantly the question is asked, "What were you thinking all that time?"

Many times in the past I had found myself inadequate to handle a given situation mentally or spiritually, but the physical drive never ceased. My *wheels kept spinning*. Now in total helplessness (and this applies to any situation in our lives), I was forced to rely on God for His strength. In a time of desperation we find that God is mightier than circumstances. "My grace is sufficient for thee; for My strength is made perfect in weakness." (2 Corinthians 12:9)

After I had given up the human fight and lay sprawled on the floor on my back, I prayed, "God, I can't do any more. You will have to take over now. I don't want to die, but if You want me to live, You will have to send me help." As I prayed I felt the security of His arms under me and about me, and it was very peaceful. Deuteronomy 33:27 says, "The eternal

God is thy refuge, and underneath are the everlasting arms."

For a long time before this illness I had begun to question my faith. It seemed almost everyone I discussed this with had experienced very traumatic emotionalism in their acceptance of Jesus Christ. It had been a complete turning around for them. Many believed this was necessary. I had never had such an experience, for my faith had been a steady, growing thing. I was wondering if this Christianity of mine was real or if I was just being smug. So I asked God this night how I stood. God assured me that my way was also acceptable — "any door open to God is the right door," He said, and I was reminded here of the Scripture: "And I say unto you, Ask, and it shall be given you; seek, and ye shall find; knock, and it shall be opened unto you. For everyone that asketh receiveth; and he that seeketh findeth; and to him that knocketh it shall be opened." (Luke 11:9-10)

It was in this stillness that I knew my true identity as His child. Continuously the words came to me, "Be still, and know that I am God" (Psalm 46:10). The room was warm and comforting with His omniscient power. Now I understood the Trinity, for here I experienced the Third Person of the Godhead — the presence of the Holy Spirit. Throughout the remainder of the night I was aware of a *gentle, blissful voice* telling me that I was not going to die. The voice was perfectly clear, and the constant assurance was overwhelming. I was told that I was going to be very sick but to *"remember* that everything will be all right again."

Remember? That *gentle, blissful voice* — that thrilling,

comforting, assuring voice — was not loud or even audible, but rather a *sense* coming from within my soul! I had heard it before! Then I *remembered* my meeting with Jesus several months earlier (the Second Person of the Godhead). Shortly after surgery I was having severe pains in my sides and legs which were eventually diagnosed as diverticulosis and had nothing to do with the surgery. But one night I was lying in bed worrying about the pain when suddenly I felt a presence in the room with me. As I looked up, a cloud-like shape was drifting across my bed and stopped directly over me. I felt as if I were being lifted and suspended in the air. In this cloud was Jesus' face — and I knew Him! I shall never forget the face. The vivid black eyes, penetrating and warm, were full of understanding. The skin was olive — like a brand new copper penny. The hair was soft, dark brown and slightly wavy. He was radiant, and as gentle as was His voice when He spoke my name. He told me that I was not to worry about myself and everything was going to be all right, that I only had to trust in Him.

I remember saying, "Thank You, Jesus," and I was in His presence for a few moments until I felt complete peace and assurance. Then it was I who let Him go. I'm sure He would have stayed longer. I lay awake for awhile hardly believing this had happened to me, but it was certainly no dream. I was not cured of the problem immediately, but all anxiety and worry were gone at the time. I thought He was talking about my immediate concern, the pain in my side. Now I know He was not. Eight months before my present predicament on the floor I had experienced, for a period of two months, what was diagnosed as depression. This was a horrible and frightening experience. Every nerve in my body was screaming. This eventually passed, and I was sure this was the answer to God's message that everything would be well again. But now I know He had been preparing me for what was yet to happen, beginning this very night.

Throughout the night I did not lose consciousness. God was in this too, for had I been unconscious so long, there could have been the danger of brain damage. My mind stayed alert, although confused, through this long terrifying night.

I heard the clock strike eight. "Everyone is stirring now and someone will find me soon," I reasoned. I had the assurance I needed that I would live, and with that knowledge help would have to come very soon. Still, I had not quite "let go and let God," for I was wondering how He was going to accomplish my rescue. When my friend left me the night before, she commented that she would check on me this morning, but what if she gave up when the telephone gave a busy signal! Who else might call or come by, and would they suspect? Perhaps the telephone company would check, since the receiver had been off the hook for most of the night. There was one lonely strike coming from that clock that seemed to echo in the stillness of the morning. It was 8:30!

Then I heard a car stop in our driveway. At last! The doorbell rang several times, and then there was a long silence. Soon I heard the car leave. Whoever this was had assumed I wasn't at home and had not suspected anything unusual, I supposed. By now my mind and body were completely exhausted.

I don't remember when the clock struck nine. Things were fading out, and perhaps I was near to unconsciousness. However, it didn't seem long until I heard a car for the second time. This time it was evident that whoever was in this car was here for one purpose and was not going to leave until sure whether I was inside the house or not.

The doorbell rang, the door rattled, and I felt relief with the concern and determination they were exercising. I recognized the voices of my companion of the night before and her husband as they called me loudly and excitedly. I learned later that she had been alarmed when she came by a few minutes earlier but had been afraid to break in. Then she called her husband at his office to join her rather than enter the house alone. Her call to me earlier that morning had not satisfied her with simply the fact that my telephone was busy. Checking with the telephone company supervisor, she was informed that the telephone was off the hook, but that no one was talking on it. Becoming uneasy, she went into action.

Without the assurance that I was continually receiving, it would have seemed doubtful to me that anyone would have suspected anything simply because my telephone line was busy. It was not unusual for me to be talking on it at this early hour of the morning. Neither would it seem unusual for me not to answer the doorbell nor for the house to be closed this particular morning, because at 9:30 (almost exactly the time I was found) I was to have boarded a plane

26

for Florida, where my husband was working. Also, it was believed that I would sleep off my illness of the night before. Yet, while I was being consoled by that *blissful voice* and assured that I was not going to die and that I would be found, my friend was also being urged by her subconscious to dismiss all practical reasoning and to check further before allowing herself to be satisfied. She said her first thought when the line was busy was, "There's nothing wrong with her this morning — she's already on the telephone"; and she was inclined to go about her busy day. This great force within her would not let her be at ease. So she got into her car and drove over. I do not believe this was a mere coincidence.

When they reached my bedroom and saw me there on the floor, they were petrified. For a moment I forgot all else but pity for those two. I could sense the tremendous impact this was making on them. I remember wanting to assure them not to worry, that everything was going to be all right. I wanted so much to transmit to them the peace that I had received.

There was no doubt in their minds that I was dead, and they said so. I was blue, my eyes were rolled back and set; there were no visible signs of heart beat or breathing, and my chest rattled. I tried so hard to tell them I was not dead, to please hurry for help, I prayed that God would let something move to show them; but nothing happened.

They ran to a neighbor's house and called the coroner and the sheriff. I was alone again. But in only seconds, it seemed, they returned with the coroner, the sheriff, and my minister, Rev. George Ross. I shall never forget the satisfaction I felt when this redheaded friend and man of God entered my room. His very presence was a great comfort to me throughout that long, tragic day. It was he who rode in the ambulance with me to the hospital. In the absence of my husband, he took over completely. He called each member of my family and met them at the hospital as they arrived separately. He also stayed with me all day and into the evening until they arrived from such long distances. They were in a state of shock, and he was certainly needed. I hope no one ever has to face any such suffering and strain without a church and a minister.

I prayed again to God that He would just let something move to show these people that I was not dead. I tried desperately to move every limb. The coroner went directly to the telephone and placed it back on the receiver. Surmising from the conversation going on around me, I was afraid he was going to call the mortuary. Somewhere, sometime, I had read or heard of this happening, perhaps in a horror movie. Certainly this was a horror scene. And the thought that I could be the next victim went through my muddled mind. Everything was an exaggerated nightmare anyway. Through the excitement he did not feel my pulse nor check my heart or my breathing. I was glad, for I alone knew that I was alive, and I didn't want time wasted getting me to the hospital.

As the coroner was walking past my inert form — and from all obvious indications my lifeless body — my left arm lifted from my side. "Thank You, dear God!" Although I could not transmit this emotion or any of my thoughts and feelings to these people around me, there are no words to describe my profound exuberance when I heard the coroner say, "She's not dead; she moved her arm." The coroner then called an ambulance. At last, things were being done! Again God had not failed!

The seriousness of the situation was profoundly evident to me again in the ambulance. Sirens can make the flesh crawl at any time, but being the victim is especially frightening. When they rolled me inside the ambulance and turned on the siren, I never felt more desperate. En route to the hospital I was pleading desperately to let it be known that I was drowning by continuously motioning to my throat with my left arm.

As all waited for the ambulance, they tried to question me. Since it was assumed that this was the effect of medication, they thought it was possible that I had taken something else or more than was prescribed. I wanted so much to tell them I had not, but I lay there listening to the discussion and questions, and I could offer no light on the subject. "Please, no questions, just do something!" Of course, there was nothing they could do except wait for the ambulance. All of the medicine bottles in the cabinet were gathered up and taken to the hospital for analysis. Even in my present state I knew that if I ever had another opportunity, unused bottles of medicine would be thrown away immediately.

To aid in the suspicion, someone among those who had gathered outside my house unwittingly informed the sheriff with the misinformation that my husband and I were separated. This gave him reason to suspect an overdose, and it went on the record to the emergency room. Because his profession takes him out of town, my husband's car is seldom at home except on weekends; so I suppose anyone not informed could easily presume this absence as permanent. I bring this up here only to show the problems we can sometimes cause when we speak without basis in fact and thus hurt our neighbor and displease God. It seems that I am constantly reminding myself of my favorite and most needed prayer: "Let the words of my mouth and the meditation of my heart be acceptable in thy sight, O Lord . . ." (Psalm 19:14). Yet, how many times I have been guilty of misdeeds without thought of the consequences!

As I have mentioned, I had been frantically trying to tell those around me that I was drowning by motioning to my mouth and throat with my hand. I learned later that they had interpreted this as my trying to tell them that I had taken something by mouth. Certainly this was a reasonable assumption. As if there were not already enough seeming evidence to convince anyone what the problem was, there was by my bedside a bottle of pills turned over with the pills spilled out. What else could they think? And I could not explain! If I could have, I would have told them that for the past few days I had been dropping things quite often. And that morning I had reached for the pills which had been prescribed for the virus, spilling them when I dropped the bottle. I still have a hole in my kitchen tile where I dropped a skillet the previous day. That is the picture that was painted for my rescuers.

Since the doctors were groping desperately for some insight, and my symptoms were exactly the same as that of a person who had taken an overdose, it was reasonable to suspect either an overdose or attempted suicide. With my body sprawled on the floor, with the medicine bottle turned over and pills spilled on the nightstand, with the information supplied outside my home, and with my constant and desperate pleading that I was drowning by pointing to my throat, giving the impression that I had swallowed something, what else could they think? Much time and suffering was spent pumping my stomach; moreover, I had to be subjected to questions over and over: "You may as well tell us what you took, because we are going to find out anyway!"

Unnecessary mental anguish was experienced. I remember a particular discussion when someone in the emergency room made the statement, "She and her husband are separated and she has been depressed." This little tidbit had already taken on new and enlarged dimensions. I shall never forget the agony I felt at not being able to defend myself, I silently questioned, "What if I die and they never know differently?" My family could even be burdened with the thought that I may have committed suicide. Many times since then I have thought how much injustice must have been written into history about people who were not around to say, "That's not the way it was."

Also, the doctor who had insisted that I tell him what I had taken was obviously unhappy because he had been pulled in on the situation. Perhaps he had better things to do than bother with a woman who, as he probably assumed, didn't want to live anyway. His language and attitude were uncalled for, and I wished so much that he would understand. This made me grateful for those around who showed sympathy and concern but did not expose this skeptical approach.

Someone in white returned to the room with results from the tests made on the medication found in my home, and stated, "There's nothing here to cause reactions such as this." "We've pumped the stomach and it's clear," said another. I shall never forget saying inaudibly, "Thank God!" when a doctor finally said, "I'm convinced it's not suicide."

3

Surrendering the "Cares of this Life"

Before the doctor could be located and get to emergency, things were looking pretty dismal, especially for my minister, who had assumed the responsibility of me. There was not a doctor to be found. I had picked a bad time to make my scene, and the hospital did not have a resident physician.

A psychiatrist, unfortunately for him, appeared in the hall. The minister knew him and insisted he do something for me. I wasn't exactly aware of everything that was going on, but I knew who the psychiatrist was, and so my thoughts were: "O Lord, I've had it!" With all the excitement over pills at home, they're now bringing in someone to try and find out why the attempted suicide. If they didn't hurry, it wouldn't make the records as *attempted.*

The next thing I knew, however, the emergency room seemed to be swarming with people.

I was told there were 22 people working on me in emergency that gloomy morning. I don't know; but

I was conscious of the room being crowded with doctors, nurses, technicians, and inhalation therapists, and there was certainly a necessary amount of excitement and commotion. I felt like dough being kneaded for bread; for I was being punched, turned, twisted, rolled, and stuck from every direction. The harassment I went through is beyond all conception, with so many trying so hard to save my life.

The talking that was going on sounded like echoes coming from inside the very walls. If you have ever watched the television series *Wild, Wild West* you will know exactly what I mean. Those characters were constantly falling into some underground trap. It was like that with me here, as though I were in a deep hole and the voices were coming from far above and around me, bouncing on and off the ceiling and the walls. They would fade out, then come on strong and fade away again.

Nevertheless I was also keenly aware of the wonderful professional care I was receiving. The tremendous knowledge, concern, and compassion were evident to me even in my present state and frame of mind, and I was grateful.

I was now aware of the presence of Dr. Albert Rees, the doctor I had seen the night before. Although he was new to me and I to him, I knew immediately that God had directed him to the scene to care for me. His superb skills and his professional manner have brought me through many a tough spot. His calmness and obvious ability in the emergency room gave me needed confidence.

By now it seemed to me that neither my body nor

my mind could stand any more. I was literally worn out. Absolutely nothing mattered any more, and I welcomed death. And death it surely was — or so it seemed to me and to those tending me, I suspected. They had worked so long and so hard and were exhausted, but they did not hesitate in their work for a moment.

There was that very fine line that I believed to be approaching death. The body becomes nothing, but the spirit is very much alive. At long last I felt a wonderful, much desired rest. I thought of my family but I knew God would care for them, and I was completely at peace. Previous to this, I had considered myself indispensable to them.

I had loved life, always enjoying the busyness and the activities in which I had participated. However, this was all of no importance to me now. I cherished my friends, but I released them also to God's care. I had found greater joy now than ever before. There were no more worries or fears, and everything prior to this moment was erased from my mind. I felt safe in God's care and sure that He had received me; then I faded away. I only hope I have emphasized sufficiently how unimportant anything of this world becomes and how easy it is to leave everything behind in God's care if one has set his house in order.

In the 21st chapter of Luke, verses 34-36, we are reminded that we must not let life overburden or overwhelm us, but that we must be ready at a moment's notice to shed it all "to stand before the Son of Man."

I do not know how long I remained in this state; but, as I had been assured more than once, death was not yet God's plan for me. I remember "coming to" and hearing voices in unison, "She's coming around, her eyes are open." I felt wonderful! For one brief moment I thought everything was behind me and that I was actually able to walk out of the hospital and go home. I was breathing fresh air. Oh, how wonderfully fresh it was! Breathing had been such an effort for so many hours before and had gradually become impossible. In fact, that had been every bit as frightening as not being able to swallow. I had struggled so hard to breathe when the inhalation therapists were working with me and insisting that I try; but I simply could not force another breath.

Soon, however, I realized that it was not I alone doing the breathing. Something very strange and uncomfortable was fastened into my mouth—something connected by a long, fat hose to a monstrous machine with all sizes of clocks and knobs on it. I didn't like what I saw or felt, for tubes were also hanging from bottles on every corner of my table and needles were stuck in me wherever they had found a vein. It was obvious that I was seriously ill. The good feeling I had experienced for one brief moment had passed, and I was feeling absolutely terrible now. There was so much pain, more than I thought I could possibly bear, over my entire body, and I was extremely cold.

From the conversation around me I knew they were getting ready to take me to the intensive care unit of the hospital. I also knew what this meant. It meant that I was so critically ill that I would have to be carefully and constantly watched.

When I was lifted from the stretcher onto the bed in my new surroundings, I was still cold—like a block of ice. The doctor was aware of this and ordered me to be wrapped with blankets. I thought they would never stop piling on blankets, and in no time at all I was feeling an extreme reverse, for I was absolutely burning up. You will hear more about this because this intense heat was something I had to contend with for several months.

The intensive care unit looked quite complicated to me. My vital signs were being monitered, and I could see lights flashing and graphs being charted at the nurses' station, which was only a few feet away. The wall between my room and the nurses' station was all glass, and a nurse paced up and down past my glass wall day and night. It was a secure feeling to know that I was being so closely observed, yet it was a frightening thought knowing why I was being observed like this. I was extremely tired. I wish I could describe the difference between the severe exhaustion I experienced then and the fatigue we complain of when we simply outdo ourselves.

Now the doctors (there were several) were busy trying to determine what was wrong with me. I could see them in conference outside the glass wall. There were several possibilities, but nothing concrete. Sometimes a few words were dropped within range of my ears. I knew my family and several friends were nearby 24 hours a day, grasping for every little bit of explanation and encouragement that was shed on the matter. Everyone felt helpless; there was so little that they could do but wait—and watch and pray. The possibility of drug intoxication (the reactions of the two different medications I had been given for the virus) had not been completely ruled out. It could be a stroke, brain tumor, encephalitis, or numerous other diseases of which I had never heard.

I was paralyzed! Shortly after I had entered intensive care I became aware of this situation. The doctor kept testing every part of my body. Total paralysis was obvious; I didn't have to be told. Yet when I would hear the word mentioned, I was terrified. I had to tell myself over and over again that they were referring to me. One hears of this sort of thing happening to other people, but it couldn't possibly be happening to me—Yvonne Wilson. I just couldn't believe it! All I could do now was to lie still, hurt, and try to reason; but absolutely nothing made any sense whatsoever.

Late that first afternoon I was struggling again for breath. The machine being used was being triggered by my own efforts; but I did not know this. I kept thinking, "I'm running out of breath; I can't possibly go on this way much longer." I heard a discussion on how long I could last on this machine. In my ignorance I thought that if and when I couldn't last any longer, it would be the end for me. Now I know that those little "clocks" were telling them exactly what I was doing, but I didn't realize that at the time. So I tried harder and harder on my own until finally the effort became too great. I told myself I just didn't care any more, for I was too tired. I remember the last breath on my own. I became unconscious again, and this time when I came to, I was hooked up to a different machine. It was bigger and appeared to be more complicated than the former one, but it was doing all the work for me.

I was rolled out of my "glass cage" constantly for some test or for X rays. Frankly, I did not like this, because I would rather have been left alone in my misery. I had begun to feel a little more security here where I was being watched so closely, and I was afraid of being taken away from this environment. However, all the equipment and machinery went with me everywhere. We could hardly squeeze through the halls or into elevators because so much and so many went along. My stretcher was always surrounded by nurses, technicians, and inhalation therapists with their portable breathing equipment, pumped by hand. They sensed my fear that their hands might tire or miss a beat, and they continually assured me of my safety. An inhalation therapist was as often as not on the stretcher with me getting through doors and other tight places because I could not take a single breath on my own. Also the lung muscles were completely paralyzed.

On the third day Dr. Rees entered my room with a surgeon. The two doctors informed me that a tracheotomy was necessary. I didn't know what that meant, but I couldn't tell them. Anyway, at this point, it didn't really matter to me. I wondered how much more I could endure. I would have much preferred that they just leave me alone, but I couldn't tell them that either. However, I had confidence in both the doctors, for Dr. Breaux, the surgeon, had performed the operation a year before. When they explained the procedure to me, I felt some better. They tilted my head and neck backward, deadened my throat, and made the incision. An endotracheal tube was installed in my throat; it extended into my lungs and was connected to the volume respirator — an automatic breathing machine for use with critically ill patients. In my case it was a matter of the lung muscles being paralyzed, thus making breathing impossible. Although it was more stable than I, this machine and I were partners for a long, long time. Every few minutes my lungs were suctioned through the trachea to clear bronchial secretions. You will be hearing more of this in following chapters, because this machine sustained my life for a total period of 287 days.

4

"He Maketh Me to Lie Down"

ROOM 553 – POSITIVELY NO VISITORS
DOCTOR'S ORDERS

Inside this room I had to learn to live, but it wasn't much of a life! In fact, it was so unrealistic that I wasn't sure if I were a human being at all. Although I was allowed no visitors (and I certainly didn't care to see anyone), my room was always crowded with necessary hospital staff, family, or with friends who from time to time relieved my family. I was experiencing double vision now and I saw two of everybody and everything. In my dense and confused condition I thought it was literally so.

Those attending me said the room was large and that it was next to the nurses' station. I agreed that the room was large because everything was so distorted to me that when those staying with me were only a few feet from my bed, it appeared to me that they were several miles away and as if the room went downhill toward them. This was very frightening because I felt they were not staying nearly close enough to my bedside. This went on for several months, but of course no one knew the full extent of the weird and distorted hallucinations from which I was suffering. I could see outlines of people and things, but I could not see enough to recognize anyone or any object. Everybody and everything, even the ceiling, appeared to be covered with a very fine net with yellow polka dots! If I would stare long enough, the yellow would turn into red.

At this time, however, my eyes were the only thing about me that would move even slightly. This was our means of communication for a long time. If I were asked a question, I was supposed to blink once for no and twice for yes. Sometimes I would become confused, at which times my blinks would mislead those poor souls who were trying to understand me.

The diagnosis was certain now. I was aware of the family and doctor outside my door in concentrated discussion. I wondered if they would tell me everything. I wasn't sure how much I wanted to be told, although I was prepared for the worst. This is why it was enlightening when Dr. Rees stood by my bedside and very calmly told me what was wrong with me and the circumstances of the illness. He told me that I would be well again, although it would take "several weeks." The assurance that I was going to live, walk, talk, and be active again sounded good to me, because I had already decided that, no matter what I had to go through, I still wanted to live. However, there were many times after this that I doubted this desire to live.

I gave much thought to the doctor's statement of "several weeks." It didn't quite add up, for if it were to be a *few* weeks, he would have said so. Therefore he must have meant a few months. I am grateful, however, that he didn't tell me "several months," because it would have seemed impossible to fight that long.

Dr. Earl Hackett, neurologist from the School of Medicine, Louisiana State University, New Orleans, had been called in on the case and had confirmed Dr. Rees' diagnosis.

I was stricken with a rare disease known as myeloradiculoneuritis, or Guillain-Barre syndrome, believed to be caused by a virus. The symptoms are proximal motor weakness and distal disturbances of the extremities. Often it follows acute viral infection. It is characterized by high protein content of the spinal fluid with little or no increase in the cells. In some instances cranial nerve palsies (facial weakness) and mental disturbances indicate the involvement of the brain as well. The nerves of the body are paralyzed, and often people die from it. One doctor explained that it's like a conduit: If you strip away the casing, the raw wires touch and short out. The sheath of the nerves is stripped, and the nerves don't conduct.

The Guillain-Barre syndrome usually paralyzes only part of the body, and the patient nearly always has some warning. However, this was not the case with me. I had no prior suspicion and I was hit fast, the paralysis descending rapidly over my entire body. The disease is tricky. It cannot be diagnosed unless there are obvious symptoms. Diagnosis is of no avail, because it runs its full course regardless, and there is no treatment for it. It is also a tremendous strain on the heart. If the patient is kept alive, however, it can be 100 percent recoverable. The victim of Guillain-Barre

43

syndrome suffers a shattering psychological impact. Taken so completely out of one's environment, it can induce schizophrenia in a person because of this emotional insecurity.

Now that we knew what I had—but because we had not heard of this disease before—my family and friends were searching every record possible to learn what they could about Guillain-Barre. Needless to say, there was little to be found, for very little is known about it. It is self-limited, usually lasting from a few weeks to several months. That was all we knew. I was given as much cortisone as possible, but it is not known if this does any good. After a period of time it had to be discontinued to prevent side effects. We were told that rest and good nursing were essential and that I should be turned often. As far as I was concerned, they couldn't turn me often enough, for I ached and my joints hurt without cessation. As soon as I was turned on one side, I was wishing to be turned again. There was never a letup from this tremendous aching and throbbing.

The constant suctioning of my mouth (because I could not swallow), my nose, and my lungs was a continuous, painful harassment. Living with the respirator was the hardest adjustment that I have experienced in my lifetime. It was frightening to me and to those staying with me. They tell me now how they would try to breathe with the rhythm of the machine, and how scared they would be when the deep breath held for a second longer than they thought it should.

It was my tired body on that hospital bed, but no part of it was functioning on its own. The noise and tempo of the breathing machine played the same loud beat over and over without intermission. I would count to the beat; I would put words to the noisy tune; I would make poetry to the rhythm. In an endless pace my very thoughts were synchronized day and night with this machine. There was no end to this nerve-racking but lifesaving device. I remember in my times of despair and pleas for help I would repeat over and over, "Oh, Lord," but it wasn't in rhythm with the machine that way and so it had to be, "Oh, Lord-ee, Oh, Lord-ee." The nearest solution I could find while fighting with the rhythm of the machine, and trying to soothe my nerves, was to set its tempo in harmony with God.

The noise from this respirator sounded loud like a train. I would almost see the wheels turning on their tracks, and I felt the motion of the train — chuga, chuga — chuga, chuga. I felt high, suspended in the air, floating out of orbit with everything out of proportion. All of this was exaggerated to me because of the extent of the physical and mental disturbances I was experiencing.

With my face and jaws paralyzed, my teeth had locked on my tongue, and until my jaws were forced open to put the feeding tube through my throat into my stomach, I wondered how long I could take the pain of my tongue.

There was the agonizing horror of not being able to talk — feeling that I just had to share this misery of mine with someone. If I could only tell them where I hurt! It was certainly not easy reconciling myself to the fact that I could not communicate by word now, and there was no positive proof that I ever would.

I learned later that until and unless I talked, they could not be sure whether or not there was brain damage. The knowing was a long, long time in coming.

With the paralysis, I felt disfigured and began to think I was a monkey. The bars on my bed were the cage. When people would come to my bed and reach down to wipe my face, I thought they were trying to feed me peanuts. I wished frantically to feel my face — just to be able to touch would have eased my anxiety, I thought. Mentally I tried, but of course my arm would not so much as budge from its position, much less lift itself up to my face. My nose and mouth were bleeding from so much suctioning, and the drainage was being mopped up with tissue. When the tissue was pulled from the boxes, the noise was so loud it hurt my ears, and each pull of tissue was in tune with the respirator. One day someone referred to the mucus from my mouth as slop. Immediately I thought I was a pig and my mouth actually felt like a snout. Inwardly I cried!

On the second day in my room the doctor had suggested that someone read to me to keep my mind occupied and off my own tragedy. My daughter chose a book from my bedside table at home and brought it to the hospital to read to me. The book was *God's Psychiatry*, by Charles L. Allen. I was sitting on my bed at home reading this book the night I became ill. Now Dana was reading the very part that had made such an impression on me that night at home. I had practically memorized it. I didn't know why, but I told myself at the time that the points made here by Charles Allen were worth remembering in order to console someone else who might be sick at some time in the future. Now I knew why this second verse of the Twenty-Third Psalm had been implanted in my mind. It was not for someone else. "He maketh *me* to lie down in green pastures; He leadeth *me* beside the still waters." (Psalm 23:2)

Charles Allen tells of being in the hospital once and feeling that he didn't have the time to waste in bed. A minister friend reminded him: "He maketh me to lie down." Allen reflects, "Sometimes God puts us on our backs in order to give us a chance to look up; 'He maketh me to lie down.' Many times we are forced, not by God but by circumstances of one sort or another, to lie down. That can always be a blessed experience. Even the bed of an invalid may be a blessing if he takes advantage of it!" Again he says, "Our visions of God come when we stop." And, "Jesus took time to be alone and pray."

"He leadeth me beside still waters." I wasn't sure I understood this part, for physically I was so hot I couldn't imagine anything so refreshing as "still waters." Yet I knew if I were to withstand my present predicament, I must know this peace. Charles Allen said that "God would not lead His children anywhere they could not go safely." So I concentrated on God's love and I practiced peace within my soul. It was not easy, but it certainly helped.

The next day Dennis, my son-in-law, began to read to me. I knew because he held a book in his hands and his mouth was moving, but I could not hear. Suddenly it was evident to me that my hearing had deteriorated to normal sounds. Dennis wasn't aware of this, but it must have seemed obvious to him that I wasn't interested, because shortly he put the book down. I don't think anyone knew I couldn't hear, because they didn't stop talking to me. Sometimes I could read their lips, but most of the time I couldn't see that well. I couldn't decide which I would rather have back—my sight or my hearing. This condition lasted for several weeks.

Another ordeal I had to tolerate was the tube feeding which combined my nourishment and cortisone. This seemed an impossible struggle! I was fed every three hours, day and night. I began to dread this immensely because I could not keep anything on my stomach. The second a drop of the feeding touched my stomach, it felt like fire and cramped me beyond all possible description. Immediately the food flushed itself on through the body. This was not only a source of great discomfort but also much embarrassment. Even at a time of such desperate illness there is still a great desire for the protection of personal privacy. The doctor was kept busy trying to find something I could take, for I had to have the nourishment. This went on and on for weeks and into months before I was actually free of cramps from the feedings. I never looked forward to these meals. Neither was I interested for a long time afterwards in food of any sort that contained eggs, milk, or sugar.

Nurses or sitters were found to watch me around the clock, and either my family or a close friend stayed with me for many months. It was frightening to be left without someone I knew. I was afraid to trust anyone strange to me. It was also difficult to find someone who would stay awake at night and watch me like they were supposed to do. Many nights I would stare at them while they slept, and this was a most frightening thing happening to me. This is when I made promises to God as never before. I lay there and prayed that they would wake. All day long I worried about the night, and all night long I kept my eyes on the window waiting for a sign of daybreak, because then Ted, my son, would be coming through the door — and then I could relax.

It was in this time of need that I promised God I would do whatever He asked of me from then on. I asked that He always keep me aware of what He had planned for me. That was a strong promise made in desperation, but I knew what I was doing — that I was placing myself in God's hands. Of course, I was unable to tell my family about the situation of the sleeping sitters. It would be two or three days before they would think to quiz me about this, and questions had to be directed to me before I could make them understand with my blinks. However, they soon learned to check every morning and consequently several sitters passed in and out my door before one was found who would stay awake. It was also apparent to me that some of the sitters didn't think I would be alive the next morning anyway. I was in such a state of shock and fear that I simply could not sleep. This inability to sleep lasted for several weeks. It was several months before the paralysis allowed my eyes to close completely.

It was the love of God, the constant care, compassion, and effort of my wonderful family, many friends, and hospital staff that made my days possible. I don't know how they did so much yet never seemed to weary.

5

The Holy Spirit Vitalizes and Takes Command of the Body

"Yea, though I walk through the valley of the shadow of death, I will fear no evil, for Thou art with me; Thy rod and Thy staff they comfort me." (Psalm 23:4)

Charles Allen prescribed the Twenty-Third Psalm as a "pattern of thinking." Lying in bed, I repeated the verses over and over until my mind became saturated with these words, as he had suggested. He also wrote, "Its power is not in memorizing the words, but rather in thinking the thoughts." Through the pain, fear, and apprehension, I was now seeing new meaning in the words of this psalm. As I thought through this fourth verse, I found it had new dimensions for me—especially for me now; for before the night on the floor of my bedroom I would not have known it in this light.

From the beginning there was difficulty in maintaining my blood pressure. Day and night the pressure was unobtainable, and I would lose consciousness. My life was constantly at a low ebb. I would know when the entire floor of nurses, supervisor, and doctor went into emergency action. I knew more than they; I knew I wasn't going to die! This reassuring voice within me continually consoled me, and I was not afraid. It is hard to convey to someone else my feeling of total lifelessness in these situations and at the same time know that I would pull through any crisis and live. I wished that I could transmit to others this reassurance. Yet I could never conquer the fear of not being watched constantly. I would panic and almost go into a state of shock when my sitters would sleep or neglect me. I knew if anything happened to me it would save much agony and setback if the nurses were made aware of the condition immediately. That is why I began to relax when they finally found someone who stayed awake and who showed concern.

"For Thou art with me; Thy rod and Thy staff, they comfort me." On that night of May 12, through emergency, intensive care, Room 553, and now at home I have come to know the power and comfort of these 13 words.

There is a spiritual sanctuary within every person. We should enter into this sanctuary when our emotions and our problems seem to be beyond us. "When you pray, go into your closet" (Matthew 6:6 RSV). The Holy Spirit is a tremendous unused spiritual power available to us at all times.

The gift of the Holy Spirit becomes available to us at the very moment that we are led to accept Christ as our Lord and Savior. Many of us are not aware of this Presence, because we do not understand what the Holy Spirit is. This is why our conduct is seldom directed by this power within us. Even with this understanding

51

and after experiencing His guidance, we still are some-times so headstrong that we fail to avail ourselves of His omnipotence.

There was a time a few years ago when our family needed to make a change. We weren't quite sure what we should do. One day as we were traveling near Dallas, Texas, a strong force within me said, "Move!" I kept tossing this about, but it seemed so right that I mentioned it to my husband. Strange, but he had been thinking along the same line and agreed with me! This would mean a traumatic change, because it would mean moving the family to another state. However, we went right ahead with our plans, plunging through each obstacle; and it was proved that this move was right for us. With the knowledge I now have, I would have known it was the Holy Spirit working through our subconscious into the conscious and directing this move. At the time I thought it was our better impulses.

We have accepted Christ, we have believed, we have practiced our faith, and Christ has accepted this Spirit-worked faith of ours. Yet we have spent our proverbial 40 years in the wilderness as we journey from Egypt to Canaan. It is when we reach the land of Canaan, when we can fathom this power to control our thoughts, deeds, and actions, that we have a *renewal* of the Holy Spirit.

It is this *renewal,* this spiritual perception, that reveals the answers to our problems. We must reach God through the words of Jesus and the Spirit dwelling within our body. Jesus said: "The words that I speak unto you I speak not of Myself, but the Father that dwelleth in Me, He doeth the works." (John 14:10)

52

Many times in my weaknesses has the Holy Spirit directed my way. But this is not easy. It takes effort to stay in harmony with the Spirit. I had told myself during those critical days that when I was up and about again, I would make a great witness, for I had experienced everything, I had been tested, and I had passed the test. However, as soon as I was thinking clearly again, there was the same old satanic nature as before. So I had to search within. There are always those two strong forces working within us — good versus evil. Therefore we can never let down our guard. It is also true that the harder we fight the evil spirit, the more he tries to permeate our lives. So we must turn from unholy thoughts and seek God's Spirit within us. We must clear the subconscious so that the conscious can convey only truth, hope, and a better way of life. Said our Lord: "I am the Way, the Truth, and the Life; no man cometh unto the Father but by Me." (John 14:6)

> This much is true: There are evil spirts in all of us. But it is no more than the baser side of our natures taking the upper hand. There is no need for incantations and the burning of candles and the ringing of bells to get rid of these personal devils. All we have to do is keep the better side of our natures in control.
>
> (*The Silver Chalice*, by Thomas B. Costain)

I still find myself taking over, thinking I can work out some problem alone. I think I have made a decision, but for one moment I think one way, then waver back the other way. Yet when I relax and turn the matter over to the Holy Spirit within me, this Spirit of God already knows my needs and is patiently waiting for me to allow Him to direct my way. "If you stray from the road to right or left you shall hear with your own ears a voice behind you, saying, This is the way; follow it" (Isaiah 30:21 NEB). Then as we follow through we hear the words, "Lo, I am with you alway." (Matthew 28:20)

People often believe that one must have an unusual or ecstatic experience to receive the Holy Spirit. This experience is considered by some to come in the form of a *sign* apparent to others, such as speaking in tongues. I do not deny that this gift is given to some and has become a tremendous breakthrough for them. However, by faith in Christ our very lives can radiate His love and His power. Then our lives become a witness for Christ; and is this not a *sign* that we have become a channel for the Holy Spirit?

I personally have not felt the need nor had the desire to speak in tongues. Yet I have had clear and undeniable communication with the Holy Spirit. With this Presence in my life, there has been no excessive emotional ecstasy. Instead there has been a quiet, warm, secure abidance in Him. When we are in tune with the Holy Spirit, He actually speaks and works through us. This divine power in one's life vitalizes and takes command of the body.

A minister speaking on the subject of the Holy Spirit was asked if he could cite an example from the Bible of a Christian who had not received this gift of tongues. "Yes," he replied, "the best example I know is Jesus Christ himself. If Jesus could have profited the world by speaking in tongues, He surely would have done so." The answer in the minister's statement was that Christ did not speak in tongues because it wasn't necessary for Him to so speak. Through the Word He imparted the Holy Spirit, who "beareth witness with spirit that we are the children of God" (Romans 8:16). It is easier to understand the Holy Spirit when we realize that we are spirit—body and spirit. "The flesh is of no avail." We were made in and are now renewed in the image of God, "for God created man in His own image" (Genesis 1:27). We are not perfect, however, and possibly this is why some have received the gift of the tongues. It is one way for helping one to come a degree closer to Christlike perfection, while other gifts are made available to others.

It seems that man has learned more about *outer space* than he has about the *inner self*. We have been given the spiritual nature of God. It is up to us to call on the Spirit's resources in faith. Through the subconscious the indwelling Spirit enters the conscious and guides us in what we are, say, do. The result is renewal.

We sing phrases such as: "Open mine eyes that I may see, Glimpses of truth Thou hast for me." The Holy Spirit has brought comfort and wisdom through many a songwriter over the decades. He continues to do so in such songs of today as "Put Your Hand in the Hand . . ."

6

My State of Quandary

One morning as mental anguish possessed me, I was aghast that so much should happen to one person. I emphatically questioned why this intolerable situation could be possible. Undoubtedly I had gone through life assuming immunity from such personal disaster. Thus I now could find no valid reason for being so totally imprisoned—shut away from the outside world which I had simply taken for granted. I spent literally hours in meditation, pondering over every conceivable sin of my past, trying to recall anything and everything that I had done wrong. Was I being punished?

The evil spirit was playing a sumptuous role with me that morning. We hassled it out much as did Job in the Old Testament. This book of the Bible had always appeared to me to be somewhat of an impossibility—almost fictitious. But I could now identify with the main character. Like Job, it was on this precipice that I was at battle with myself. I was in favor with God; He had assured me of this by His presence that night on the floor. Now I was to face the accumulation of things that I had not relinquished: self-centeredness, little jealousies, judging of others, inability to forgive, and more.

Then I would reason that my sins were inconsequential compared to the sins frowned on by society, or compared to the sins of people who are completely indifferent to any form of religion. They can take it or leave it alone, yet there never appears to be any indication of real suffering. So again I was confronted with the enigma: Why me?

Guilt haunted me for venturing into this state of quandary. I knew God would reprove my nurturing such thought, because the Bible clearly tells us, "Your heavenly Father . . . makes His sun rise on good and bad alike and sends the rain on the honest and the dishonest" (Matthew 5:45 NEB). "There must be no limit to your goodness, as your heavenly Father's goodness knows no bounds." (Matthew 4:48 NEB).

I knew also that any form of indulgence in sin is detrimental. Eugenia Price says in her book *Make Love Your Aim,* "Too many people 'gossip' under the guise of being truthful." The apostle says: "It [tongue] is a small member but it can make huge claims" (James 3:5 NEB). Speaking of anger, the Bible tells us, "He that is slow to anger is better than the mighty, and he that ruleth his spirit than he that taketh a city" (Proverbs 16:32). I believe these and all other of our seemingly insignificant but toxic emotions are often hard to shed because, for one thing, they seem to come so easily and naturally for us. It seems we can spend a lifetime with our inner human pollutions and never come to terms with them. This is partly because they become habits, and habits are hard to break. They are hard to recognize and to face objectively. I have certainly not conquered all my human imperfections. Does one ever? Should this stigma deter one from being a witness for Christ? No, I do not believe so. With God's grace and abiding love we can continually improve. "Of myself I can do nothing, but through Christ's presence and power within me I do all things," reads a paraphrase of Philippians 4:13. Someone has said that when we can't go back and we can't go on, then we must go through. It is true that if we all waited for Christlike perfection before we did anything, God's work here on earth would suffer.

While struggling with this conundrum I had a visitor whose appearance (though he did not realize it) was most timely. He was Rev. Robert King from another denomination in Lafayette. I knew Rev. King and his gracious wife, and about their strong conviction of God, His love and power. I knew that also they had experienced proof of God's miracles.

That morning as he stretched his arms to resemble a cross—one arm extending backward and one forward, Rev. King quoted this Scripture: "Forgetting those things which are behind, and reaching forth unto those things which are before, I press toward the mark . . . ." (Philippians 3:13)

I thought it rather strange that he should quote this particular Scripture to me on that very morning when I was lying there so sick. I was trying to forget the past and I certainly could not see any future. Why not something consoling, in sympathy with my present state? Why didn't he give me an answer to why I was in this muddle of illness and confusion in the first place? I did not dwell on this though because there was a mystery about the presence of this man this morning and I was sure that God had sent him with this message.

This Scripture stayed with me the 10 and a half months I remained in the hospital. I could not remember the exact quotation or even the Scriptural reference, but that was the first thing I looked up when I was able to use the Bible.

This was my consolation concerning the perplexities haunting me that morning: "Forgetting those things which are behind . . . ." (I was reminded of Lot's wife. The two angels appeared before Lot and insisted that he make haste to take his wife and two daughters out of the city of Sodom before they be consumed in the iniquity of the city. "Look not behind thee," they commanded. But Lot's wife looked back and she became a pillar of salt.) The apostle goes on, ". . . and reaching forth unto those things which are before, I press toward the mark . . . ." I knew that before our lives can be of any substance, we must accept Christ's forgiveness as a fact and concentrate on the future. We cannot harbor negation. As we gain a consciousness of Christ, we lose all thoughts of condemnation; otherwise we live a life of destruction. To inwardly torture ourselves is an insult to our Creator. Sometimes, however, questioning is the beginning of spiritual understanding. At all events, St. John writes: "If we confess our sins, He is faithful and just to forgive us our sins, and to cleanse us from all unrighteousness." (1 John 1:9)

Once again I quote from *The Silver Chalice*. Luke

told the character Adam ben Asher, "I was denied the privilege of seeing Him, but it would make no difference if He had performed no miracles at all. It is what He taught, Adam ben Asher. He brought to us the sublime truth that our God is the God of charity and forgiveness and that we may be redeemed and washed of our sins by the blood that was spilled on Calvary."

The above is saying to me that if Christ had not chosen to perform miracles for me, I would still know that He is truth — that Christ died for my sins and His plan for my life is happiness and success. It is only in Christ that I find my security.

Shortly after my visitor had left, my son-in-law came to stay with me. While making one-sided conversation he asked me if I felt my illness was brought about as punishment. I was able to truthfully blink "no." With conscience cleared of inner turmoil, I was thinking positively now.

I was entranced with this manifestation of putting all things behind and foreseeing a future of health and happiness. I felt that this was approaching the place where we "pick up our cross and follow Him." I wanted to share my enlightenment with others; but I was a long way from telling anyone. Someday I would write a book! I didn't know how, but I knew I must try. So God used Rev. King as the instrument through whom I received my initial desire to attempt this book.

The thought of putting my experiences on paper persisted, although I felt inadequate for such a task. Another blessing was soon afforded me, however, to make me more confident that the impact of God's plan was in this effort. This came when out of the clear blue a friend said to me, "You're going to write a book, and I am going to be your secretary." I couldn't answer her then, but we each stored our plans until I was able to exert the effort necessary. Getting started presented a problem—or so it seemed. Since I couldn't write, I tried dictation on a dictating machine, but my speech was still too sluggish to be understood and I would tire too easily. Then one day I experimented with an oversize pen and discovered that I could achieve a somewhat legible handwriting by forcing it between my fingers and maneuvering my wrist. With a feeling of success I went to work.

In my contention that I was not being punished, I do not mean to say we do not reap the results of our deeds—good or bad. When we use good judgment and we obey divine guidance, we can expect to reap a corresponding harvest. On the other hand, if we stick our finger into the fire, we are certainly going to get burned. We are not punished of ourselves, but by ourselves.

We know that Jesus died on the cross that our sins may be forgiven, but His blood did not erase all the consequences of our sin, such as suffering and physical death. Neither did His death take away our will to sin. It is not God's intention to destroy the will to make our own decisions in anything we do, whether constructive or destructive. It is our privilege and our moral responsibility to choose. We must, however, admit our evil ways and be obedient to God's love for us.

For the Lord corrects and disciplines every one whom He loves, and He punishes, even scourges,

every son whom He accepts and welcomes to His
heart and cherishes.

You must submit to and endure for discipline.
God is dealing with you as with sons; for what
son is there whom his father does not train and
correct and discipline?

Now if you are exempt from correction and
left without discipline in which all share, then
you are illegitimate offspring and not true sons.
(Hebrews 12:6-8 AB)

We have examples of the result of our own follies
in the early makings of American history. Soon after
the Revolutionary War our government, under the
Articles of Confederation, had no president. No
changes could be made in the articles unless every
state agreed. This was an impossibility, partly because
some states were jealous of each other. For example,
the people in New York thought that those from Con-
necticut and New Jersey who sold wood and food in
New York were enemies who carried away money from
the city. Their jealousies and revengefulness kept
them from trading with each other, thus causing
heavy taxes. In the state of Massachusetts there was
a little war named after the leader, Daniel Shays, and
known as Shays' Rebellion, which was brought about
because the people refused to obey state laws.

In *Psychology, Religion and Healing* Leslie D.
Weatherhead says that if the early church had associated herself "with science and given it her support,
at the same time maintaining her own spiritual temperature and opening the Kingdom of Heaven to all
believers, who knows what miseries of disease and

illness might have been warded off from subsequent generations? But, although the Church officially associated herself with the healing of the sick, she disapproved of the method of the scientist."

Annual expenditures for legal alcoholic beverages for the year 1972 reached nearly 25 billion dollars. This does not include moneys spent on advertising by various media, nor does it include moneys spent on medical and psychological research and treatment centers necessary as a result of the problem of alcohol and drug addiction. Think of the money spent on illicit drugs, horse racing and other forms of gambling, pornography, R and X rated movies, and many that are rated PG! If a portion of this money were directed toward medical research, we should undoubtedly know more about the heart, cancer, and many other diseases, including the Guillain-Barre syndrome.

I have been asked how a God who loves us can allow so much suffering. Is it possible that our misfortunes are not of God's own doing, but rather the consequences of a world committed to sin? God asked, "Who is this whose ignorant words cloud My design in darkness?" (Job 38:2)

7

Surrender of Self

"Pray for one another" (James 5:16 NEB). It has been this form of prayer that has lifted me and my illness up to God and His loving care from the very moment my tragedy was known to others and throughout the entire painstaking ordeal to my present state. I am blessed and grateful for these incessant prayers for my complete recovery.

Sometimes we are too ill or too depressed to pray for ourselves. We have absolutely no control of our faculties. Everything is completely out of our hands. Most of the time throughout the months spent in the hospital this was my dilemma. It is in this situation, when we are too ill or too disturbed to pray for ourselves, for our family, or our friends, that the thing left for us to do is to take Jesus' promise literally: "And be assured, I am with you always, to the end of time" (Matthew 28:20 NEB). We must be still within and proclaim the presence and power of Christ. Then we can be channels through which God can do His healing. Said Jesus to two blind men, "According to your faith be it unto you." (Matthew 9:29)

It is amid our need that intercessory prayer gives us a glorious vision of God's infallible power. My own church and its many prayer groups were continuing in constant prayer for me. Other churches in town of all denominations were meeting, all in special prayer. Churches, prayer groups, and individuals in cities over the country were praying for my recovery. One friend in Missouri called her church when she heard of my illness. The church has a special prayer room, and someone is in prayer for people and their needs around the clock.

These special petitions were heard by God and they were answered. Because of these prayers God was able to sustain my faith through every crisis in His promise that I would live. I had excellent medical attention, but prayer support was also God's proficient gift. Sometimes these intercessory prayers were answered instantaneously, while others are still being answered. I recall one particular time when a friend asked her Sunday school class to pray for my hands, that they might show some sign of movement. I had used my hands so much in crafts, painting, sewing, and cooking that the fear of not using them again was a source of worry for many and certainly for myself. The very next morning, after this special prayer in that Sunday school class, my fingers moved a little. We knew this was in answer to their prayers. I need not say how excited we were to witness this miracle.

Since I was allowed no visitors, notes were left on my door, sometimes by people I didn't know, telling me they were praying for me. There was a deep feeling of peace and satisfaction in knowing that others were truly concerned and neither hesitated nor neglected my need in their prayers. They seized the opportunity of being a channel through which God could help me to grow spiritually and physically.

When I could pray, I often found myself praying for someone else near my room. Tragedy was all about me; and it seems I was constantly aware of someone in worse condition than I. There was my family — how they needed my prayers! I made feeble efforts to pray that God would give them strength and peace of mind, and most of all I thanked Him for them. The only concrete thing I could do was to turn them and their burdens over to God. I was too sick to run the show for Him; although I must admit I didn't understand how they could weather so much, either physically or emotionally.

After he could leave me, Dan was on the road back and forth from work to my bedside. His responsibilities have not yet ceased, although they are now at a somewhat easier pace. Dennis stayed as long as his work would permit (he took the night shift too!). Then he had to be separated from Dana and the baby for the rest of the summer. This was especially hard for Dana because Kyle, our only grandson, was just 9 months old. My neighbor kept him every afternoon while she stayed with me at the hospital. That is what I call a neighbor! Ted, then 19 and a freshman in college, dropped out of school for an entire year and assumed the responsibility of my care in the hospital and at home until the fall session started. He was a giant!

It was through my own children, and the young people who cared for me at the hospital, that I was made aware of their youthful capabilities and their great response to human suffering.

The going has been rough, but we have stood up under the stress and strain and have grown closer to God and to each other because of our awareness of God's compassion in our times of need.

One afternoon a prayer was said over my bed that I shall never forget, for I have never felt the presence of God more completely than on this occasion. The prayer was offered in a language I did not understand. My minister brought a visiting mission worker, Senora Ester de Rossel, from Santiago, Chile, to visit me. Senora de Rossel prayed a long and moving prayer for me, all in Spanish. I did not know a word she said, but the hospital room was filled with His presence. There was a magnetic power around my bed that left me no doubt but that He too was there. This lady, who has done so much for the San Ramon Methodist Mission and for other churches in that area, without a doubt has a direct line to the Lord.

The very use of the word "Our" when we pray "Our Father" encompasses the desire to pray for others. For He is not exclusively your Father nor mine — but *ours*. So, when we pray "Our Father" we are actually practicing intercessory prayer.

Most of my own prayers in those early days were those of begging and pleading with God for mercy. I wanted instant healing! Being paralyzed, so completely helpless, was repugnant to my very nature, and I was convinced I could not tolerate this very much longer. There were some who had consoled me by saying that paralysis would leave my body as fast as it had overtaken me. I wanted to believe them and so I prayed, "Dear God, let me be normal *tomorrow.*" Within a few hours' time my whole life had been interrupted by this illness; and I knew if God wanted to, He could heal me just that fast. After all, had He not instantly cured the paralytic whose friends had lowered him through the roof? The Gospel writer states, "When Jesus saw their faith . . . ." (Mark 2:5). I had that faith! I believe that the New Testament miracles can be just as effective today as they were when Christ walked the earth, for He said, "I am with you always." His dying on the cross and His departing according to the flesh did not rob us of His explicit power and mercy. Again I would rationalize: Peter's own mother-in-law was cured of a fever. The account reads, "And when Jesus was come into Peter's house, He saw his wife's mother laid, and sick of a fever. And He touched her hand, and the fever left her; and she arose and ministered unto them" (Matthew 8:14-15). If only He would do this for me! He surely *could.* I was consumed with a desire for instant healing. For days I would let nothing enter my thoughts to unshackle these hopes. I felt I could not endure the pain much longer; so this was going to be my salvation.

I was aware of God's messages, and He never led me to believe I would be healed soon. In fact, He tried to steer me away from these intrusions of false hope, but I refused to listen. I would pray, I would make promises, and then I would listen for His reassurance of quick healing; but it did not come. Instead, day after day, it seemed that what He was constantly saying to me was, "Be still, and know that I am God" (Psalms

46:10), and "I will be with thee; I will not fail thee, nor forsake thee" (Joshua 1:5). But I wanted more, and so for days I simply would not relinquish such an irrational hanging on to straws.

While praying for instant healing, there was always that *gentle blissful voice* telling me that this was not the way it would be and that I could and would, without doubting or blaming God, tolerate what I must. But I desperately felt that I could not endure more; so I refused to listen to the Christ within me. I insisted on clinging to my determination that God could do for me what He did for Peter's mother-in-law. Now, there are those who will question this. They may say that it was my lack of faith that deprived me of faster healing than I have received. This constant reminder that my wishes would not always be granted exactly as I desired concerning immediate healing could be construed as negative thinking; that if I had possessed enough faith, it would have happened. However, it was not this way by any means. The *voice* was definite; it was in no way negative or of a sinful nature. It was a message from God. I firmly believe that faith has a real restoring power. Therefore it was not a matter of losing faith in God. I am still positive that He can mend nerves and strengthen muscles. I do not attempt to predict how or when, but I do expect that He will.

Then came the day that I learned the total surrender of prayer. I don't remember the date nor the time of day, but I shall never forget the moment. I had always prayed with earnest fervor and persistence for the things I thought that I needed. However, answers and solutions had not always become available as I felt they surely should. I could never understand this.

Several years ago, when our children were quite small, my husband suffered a very severe coronary thrombosis. After a couple of years in and out of the hospital because of his heart, he had a serious automobile wreck which confined him to the hospital and to the bed for another year. Things went from bad to worse over a period of a few years. There was a shortage of money and I found myself praying for the next meals. In those prayers I would ask God for food and then I would practically plan the menu for Him. I suppose I was afraid He didn't know the value of nutrition. You see, I had not learned to fully trust in His wisdom. His vision is eternal and encompasses the past, present, and future for our ultimate good; although I knew this, I was short on patience.

With my own illness now, there were still no signs of improvement. I was getting weaker, my blood pressure continued to drop, and my life was still in danger. The paralysis was not relenting one bit.

The nourishment, slowly poured through the tube in my mouth, was a constant irritation to my stomach. Because of the pain and swelling it caused, I dreaded for the nurses to administer these feedings. The heat I have mentioned before was unbearable. Someone stood over me almost continuously sponging me off with cool cloths. Yet my body felt like ice to the touch, and everyone else in the room was freezing. Because of this intense heat from which I was suffering and the sensitivity of my skin, I could not stand to have even a sheet touch my body. I could hardly endure the affectionate patting and rubbing that I received from those trying to show their sympathy. They were not aware of my sensation, and I was unable to scream! I understood that this was the only way they had of showing their compassion and love for me, and that carried me through the agony. My arms were sore from so many needles and my skin was sensitive to every touch. My joints throbbed and ached. I shall never forget the itching! My eyes itched, my nose itched, my ears itched. In fact, the itching was continuous on one spot of my body or another—actually, most of the time, every inch of me itched at the same time. If only I could have talked! I would certainly have directed all that patting energy into scratching. Because of the constant rashes, my doctor was grateful that I could not relieve the itching by scratching—but, oh, how I wished I could scratch! Can you imagine going almost a year without scratching? I still had not adjusted to the breathing machine. Finally, when the needles would not stay in my veins to supply the necessary artificial life substances, it became necessary to do a brachial cutdown under my right arm and insert a tube to take care of this problem. Time was running out before the doctor arrived to do this surgery, because the veins in my arm would not support the needle, and one moment without the needle would be fatal. For a short period, while waiting for the surgeon, the nurse was forcing the needle into position. I could sense her anxiety.

This operation involved inserting a tube into the incision in my arm and connecting the other end of it to a bottle suspended over my head. Constantly the tube would become snarled with kinks, and a nurse would spend a great deal of time tediously correcting this malfunction. When the fluid did not flow properly, I would become extremely nervous.

As previously indicated, I had tried to plan my own healing — at least as to the time element, and it was not working. Finally I simply said: "Thy will be done." Immediately I felt complacence and mental relaxation. I was sure that healing had started and I knew that my situation, so intensely complex, would somehow pass, but in God's own way and time. I knew that you cannot interfere with God's scheme of things no matter what the condition may be. "We know that all things work together for good to them that love God, to them who are the called according to His purpose" (Romans 8:28). Although I could see no good at this crucial point, I was aware of a divine presence within me that was in itself an answer to all those intercessory prayers. I had peace of mind.

It was not long before the catheter was removed; in fact, it was on the very day that placing an indwelling catheter involving an opening into the stomach was under consideration. This was another miracle, for it was explained that the outcome of this catheter often requires future surgery to remove scar tissue. For this reason this surgery had been postponed as long as it was felt advisable. My stomach was beginning to tolerate the feedings a little better; there were meager signs of improvement, but of course I was still not "out of the woods."

This surrender of self, this acceptance of "Thy will, not mine," was the greatest revelation I had ever before experienced. I have said these words to God a hundred times when someone else was concerned, even my own family; but to actually say, "Thy will" concerning myself and for the very first time sincerely mean it—and to understand the total surrender I had made by these two seemingly simple but faith-filled words—was indeed the moving of a mountain by means of a faith like a grain of mustard seed.

The persistent, day-by-day practice of prayer results in individual spiritual growth. When we are involved in prayers of intercession, we are growing spiritually. Prayer in any form is the exercising of our faith, otherwise we would be wasting words. Prior to His miraculous healings it is repeatedly said: Jesus "seeing their faith . . . ." This implies the prayers of others. When He healed the paralytic at Capernaum He must have seen the faith and heard the hopeful prayers of the friends who lowered the sick man through the roof. It was the faith of others that Jesus observed before performing the miracle of raising the daughter of Jairus from the dead. It was a father's faith that our Lord noted at the healing of a demon-possessed son. This father felt incapable of possessing sufficient faith and asked Christ to "help me where faith falls short" (Mark 9:24 NEB). After this healing Jesus told His disciples, "There is no means of casting out this sort but prayer" (Mark 9:29 NEB). Here the disciples had asked Jesus why they had been unable to heal the boy. Jesus was telling them they were lacking in faith and prayer for this particular healing.

We must recognize the fantastic medical knowledge, skills, and great scientific discoveries and medicines available to us. Our good doctors are certainly a gift of God, who uses them as instruments for healing. There are doctors who put their faith in science only, yet they perform marvelous healings. This proves that God does His works whether the person administering the medicine has the proper prospective or not. Here again the faith of others is manifest; God gives it power to act alongside and through the healing arts.

Prayer is not only an exercise of our faith but also an acknowledgement of Christ. He said that we should "acknowledge Him in all things." Some ask, "If God knows all, and if God's will is already for our good, why bother to pray?" Prayer does not change God, whose will is already for our good; but it does ask God to make us receptive to the good that God intends for us.

Then prayer is in a sense cooperation with God. Man's refusal to cooperate with God's purpose in our lives, to use the gifts which we have received (and everyone has some gift), to relax in His will is to expose his disbelief. Such attitudes can limit God's activities and close the door to His plan for our lives and for the scheme of things involving others whose lives could be made more magnificent. "And He did *not* many mighty works there because of their unbelief." (Matthew 13:58)

Here then is the formula for prayer which I have found: "And whatever you pray for in faith you will receive" (Matthew 21:22 NEB). This is God's promise, and we should proclaim His truth. Sometimes our prayers begin with self-centeredness. We should not let this deter our progress, however, for God is used to meeting us at this rather inept beginning in our prayer life. We must realize, though, that we are truly asking for God's will in our needs. We are seeking the path that He has planned for us and not what we think we want. We must pray in faith for this fulfillment. We may claim health, happiness, and peace, assuming that this is God's will. These gifts may not come in the form or manner in which we are asking; we should not plan the direction of His will. To do so is taking things out of His hands and trying to be self-sufficient. We must bear no bitterness concerning His will.

"Nevertheless not as I will, but as Thou wilt" (Matthew 26:39). We do not always know God's will, and we certainly cannot always expect immediate knowledge of His will; but His will is evident in His overall plan, and we must completely surrender to His will. This is where we practice our faith and patience. It is a pious attitude to accept negative conditions, saying that "God has willed it so." God wills that we think and act in the knowledge that His purpose for our lives is only good, and He expects us to cooperate with the divine law by the strength His own Holy Spirit imparts. It is only with this positive attitude that we can declare, "Thy will be done."

Only those who rest in God's will are really secure. It is in this total commitment that we find peace of mind, strength and courage, and obedience to "His will."

8

Attitude of Thankfulness

It was one of those evenings when everything seemed so futile that suddenly I thought I felt a little trickle of saliva go down my throat. Was it possible that I had swallowed? They had said that eventually I would, but I had often wondered. It had been such a long time, and such a grotesque unreality. I really didn't know what to expect. For all those months that stuff had boiled up in my throat. It reminded me of hot dish water, for it was hot and the taste was most unpleasant to say the least. I use the word "unpleasant" for the lack of a better word to describe this nauseous taste that had stayed with me all this time. In the early days when everything was so out of proportion I remember comparing this bizarre affliction to a volcano. I felt as if hot, molten lava and steam were gushing forth from my throat with the same angry gust.

Here I lay, unsure, but possibly swallowing again. The nurses tried a drop of ice water. Still I wasn't sure, but I believed that I swallowed it. This encouraged further testing by giving me more ice water and later broth with an eyedropper. A bit of the liquid would seep down my throat, but the rest had to be suctioned from my mouth. While trying to swallow, I had to concentrate very hard because I did not actually remember where my throat was nor in which direction the liquid should go — up or down. I would confuse my throat with my nose; consequently I was as often as not pushing the water up my nose. Then as the sensation of feeling in my throat began to return, I could feel the broth or water seeping down, and I was conscious of how to swallow again. The feeling in my throat had been a long time returning and it seemed like something entirely new to me. I only wish that I could describe the perception I had of each new thing as all these feeling sensations returned over my body — feelings that I had forgotten, or at least in many cases I remembered having them but had forgotten what they were like. Finally after all those months the unreal was happening: I was beginning to feel like I was joining the human race again. It's magnificent how God handles every minute detail.

We worked hard with this swallowing process and every ounce was charted. Finally the time came when I was able to prove to my doctor that I could consume two quarts of liquids in a day. It was then that he removed the feeding tube from my stomach, while reminding me that failure to maintain the consumption of this quantity of liquid each day would warrant inserting a tube again. That tube must have been 20 feet long — I thought they would never get to the end of it. Everyone was always excited when any tube about me could be eliminated. That meant improvement, and any trace of improvement concerning me traveled fast throughout the hospital. The hospital personnel and numerous townspeople were keeping track of my progress, for, after all, it had not been expected. By all standards I shouldn't be alive!

For all these months I never lost the desire for food, that is, for something I could get my teeth into — something besides that sweet, chalky (but nourishing) conglomeration they kept pouring down that tube. They insisted that I couldn't taste it because it was going directly to my stomach through the tube. I wondered if they had ever heard of or experienced regurgitation. Then when the broth was given it was like T-bone steak to me! Enough salt could not be applied to the food for a long, long time to satisfy my hunger for it.

Thanksgiving Day was D-day for my first solid food. A friend sent me a Thanksgiving dinner. That was a real adventure! Someone had to feed me, of course, as was done for sometime even after I came home. After my wrist became strong enough, my occupational therapist made a brace to put on my hand. With this brace, by inserting the eating utensil in a little pocket, I fed myself. The same procedure was used for my toothbrush. After 15 months I was able to brush my teeth again with this contraption. For so much, I have infinite reason to be thankful.

Going back several months before I began to swallow, when the distortion and the heat were so intense, there was difficulty in adjusting to my new environment. The hospital was another world for me. My doctor and others were concerned about the brick wall just outside my window towering high enough to restrict my view of the sky and to completely obscure any view of trees or vegetation of any kind. They were worried about the psychological effect this could possibly have. I was able to endure this situation better than even I expected. But it was in God that I found my security. I continuously reminded myself of the Scripture from Philippians 4:11 RSV: "I have learned, in whatever state I am, to be content." This was a practice I had learned many years before, and I was glad that I had it to draw on now. I tried hard to practice this in those early days of my illness and, although I am not always successful, I still find satisfaction in these words of Scripture. I think I have achieved a greater state of contentment.

One day my doctor had me transferred to another room where the view was better. I was desperately uncomfortable there. The room was smaller, crowded, and the air conditioner didn't function properly, contributing to the intense heat from which I was already suffering. Imagine that! I should have much preferred a deep-freeze! However, that wasn't the only reason for my exasperation. The room and drapes were rose-beige. With the sun shining on them, they appeared to me to be a hot, shocking pink. This vivid color, exaggerated by the sun, hurt my already weak eyes, gave me a headache, and made me very nervous. Sensing my intolerance of this situation, Ted started the procedure of getting me back to the room I had left, where the walls and drapes were a cool, restful green. This accomplished, I was much happier. I have seen that beige-colored room since, and it doesn't appear possible that the color could have been so painful to my eyes.

Those days with so much suffering, with such complete immobility, looking and feeling so gaunt, so unlike a mortal, seem like a bad dream now. But the memory of them reminds me to pray with *thanksgiving*.

Someone has said that it isn't nearly so hard hitting rock bottom if we already have it padded so we can bounce back. Even when we are on rock bottom we should not focus on adversities. It is profoundly true that God will protect us from burdens beyond our endurance. There have been many times when I have tried to discount this promise of God's because I have wondered how much more He thought I could stand, both during illness and during other adversities of life. However, regardless of wistful thinking I do believe this, and it has proved true to me time after time.

I am convinced that there is no pain "under the sun" (to appropriate a phrase from the Book of Ecclesiastes) to equal that of heartbreak. Real hurt is when parents see their children suffer or die, or when children have shown disrespect for their parents or violated God's law in other ways. When husband or wife has been unfaithful to the other, many lives can be scarred. When parents do not set the proper standard and fail to live exemplary lives, children have a hard time understanding and knowing what is expected of them. Life is a mystery — we do not always understand the whys — but somehow we plunge right through our sorrows and come out with love, understanding, and forgiveness. We can remember the triumphant moment that God showed us forgiveness.

I have been able to endure my own illness with some degree of patience only because of God's presence in my life. He has also made available to me, during my illness and convalescence, people who have been patient, understanding, and loyal. Again, I pray with *thanksgiving.*

When we do not seem to receive results from our prayers, and when the inharmonious situation persists and our problems do not seem to be resolved, we may be tempted to become remorseful or resentful, and we so readily become impatient. Perhaps our prayers have been a one-way street. We have not actually acknowledged the omnipresence of Christ when we pray without completely relinquishing our petitions to Him. Thus we feel a sense of failure. In my personal prayer life, I find that beginning my prayers with thanksgiving makes a difference. It makes me more humble in preparation for a petition to God. Acknowledging our abundances in thanksgiving makes us more receptive to the riches inherent in Him; also we are opening doors for receiving more blessings. In Colossians 4:2 we read: "Continue in prayer, and watch in the same with thanksgiving." When we sincerely thank God for our blessings we find they outnumber the things we seek of Him. I am ashamed to admit that there have been times in my life when I have asked myself, "What blessings?" However, if we have enough stamina to resist this satanic impulse that thrives in the crevices of our weak souls—if we are *watchful*—then blessings are seen.

Prayer is not a one-way street, but rather a three-way open highway to God: thankfulness, seeking, receiving. When we have waited on the Holy Spirit to direct our ways we can be certain that we have already received God's good in what we have asked. I was made aware of this promise very recently (since first writing this chapter, in fact). Early one morning as I was praying specifically for God to heal my hands, there came forth from within me the words "Thank You" before I could finish my petition and without thought on my part. I knew then that I would receive God's good as far as my hands were concerned. To prove this further, while working on this chapter, I have discovered that I could type — certainly not with my old style and speed, but it is amazing how well I do. One month ago I tried and could not get the paper in the typewriter, much less set the spacing, *et cetera*. Now in my own crude but prodigious way I am able to do all that.

We are all God's children and we are all recipients of His great abundance, often without asking. Such is His great love for us. Never a day passes that He has not blessed us in some way that we have not anticipated. And more often than not, most of us, I'm sure, fail to give Him credit. After reading *God's Smuggler*, by Brother Andrew, ingratitude became a stark reality to me, namely, my failure to realize and appreciate my freedom to worship. In America worship is so simple, and yet we fail to take advantage of this opportunity. Reading this book made a permanent impression on me concerning the difficulty of people in Communist countries to worship God.

I suppose it is because it happens to be that season of the year, Thanksgiving Day, that makes thanksgiving so prevalent in my mind at this particular time. I am reminded with gratitude of the distance I have traveled since the same holiday one year ago when I had solid food for the first time and when I was so completely incapacitated.

Just this week my therapist discovered new muscles working in my legs. The hamstrings and the ankles are obviously regenerating. The thought of muscles returning so that I can walk again is very encouraging. When I was released from the hospital and began my *outpatient* therapy program I had to be strapped to a tilt table. The intricate muscles and ligaments in the hands and fingers are the slowest returning because they are so tiny and so numerous. Until the average laymen is personally involved, one cannot imagine the skills and benefits received from this relatively new field of treatment for crippling diseases of every nature. The therapists at the rehabilitation center as well as those therapists working with me during the extremely difficult months as an *inpatient* in the hospital have striven with absolute determination to see me completely healed.

In order to keep the joints from being frozen by the loss of muscles and the lack of activity, physical therapy was started in the hospital as soon as possible. I was exercised three times a day for 15 minutes at a time. How I dreaded these treatments because they were so very painful! The breathing respirator made exercising difficult. Any movement of the body was likely to make the endotracheal tube turn in my throat, causing genuine pain. However, the therapy was an absolute necessity, and so I tolerated the agony. Those staying with me were experiencing about as much mental suffering as I was undergoing physical suffering. Usually they would turn their backs or leave the room to cry. My, how I wished I could leave the room! I could and did cry, but no one knew because there was no expression to show my real emotions. Just as soon as the therapist could get a limb going in one direction, he would start trying for a different direction. This was so excruciating that I didn't always feel it worthwhile. At these painful moments I was sure I would be satisfied with a minimum of movement. For instance, I had never realized the arm moves in so many directions. I would have been satisfied if the therapist had stopped once he had achieved the movement of my arm in the direction of my mouth. As I have said, I never lost the urge to eat. After only a few days in the hospital I began to be hungry. It seemed that the only time the film that seemingly covered my eyes, distorting my vision, ever cleared up was when they flashed food commercials on the television set in my room. They nearly drove me insane! And those cold-drink advertisement songs with the ice clinking—I was so hot and thirsty! I was also in misery when anyone even looked like he was going to eat in my room. People soon detected this and discontinued the practice. I didn't want to defeat the possibility of eating again. Neither did I like being fed like a baby. Sometimes I found this to be very humiliating, and so I would suffer almost anything to be able to feed myself again. Other than that, I was sure I could live without the other movements. Thank goodness, the therapist didn't heed my pleas!

While in the hospital, after I was able to talk (and

disagree now and then) as well as eat solid foods, my therapist insisted that no one could possibly dislike beef heart or tongue, if it were prepared properly. This is where I disagreed. He guaranteed that he would personally see to it that I would be afforded the opportunity to eat these dishes before I left the hospital. As much as I was hoping he would forget, he kept his part of his promise—the part pertaining to beef heart. I'm still waiting for the tongue! One evening he surprised me with the most appetizing dinner I had tasted in a long time. He told me that he had his grandmother, who really knew how, to do the cooking. When we think of south Louisiana, or "Cajun" cooking, we immediately associate this with fantastic seafood dishes such as shrimp jambalaya or perhaps crawfish etouffee. However, this was another version of a typical Cajun dinner. The beef heart was stuffed with all sorts of good things. It was delicious and melted in the mouth. There were stuffed potatoes, white beans, and homemade bread. Naturally there was rice with a delightful gravy made from a roux and scrumbles of beef heart. No Cajun meal is complete without native-grown rice with a roux "passed over it." It was delicious, and I didn't have to worry about all those calories because I had lost something like 40 pounds the first few weeks of my illness.

Although concentration on physical therapy is paramount at this stage of one's healing, mental therapy needs to be focused on thanksgiving. I am thankful for an effective physical therapy program and the wonderful good it has done. I am grateful for all the fine medical attention received and for the healing that proves its excellence. I am so thankful for the healing that I have received as God's answer to prayer. There have been times of specific healing as a direct result of special prayers for some particular phase or symptom of illness. These have been too obvious to deny. In the preceding chapter I told about my hands moving within a short time after a Sunday school class prayed for this very thing to happen. Once when a ladies' prayer group at my church prayed especially for my legs, the hamstrings became obviously improved that very afternoon — at approximately the hour the prayer group met. Two weeks ago, early one Sunday morning, I felt the presence of the Holy Spirit directing me to ask for special prayers that muscles I needed for balance would return and be strengthened. I tried to argue that I shouldn't bother anyone at this early hour. However, I could not resist and I called two friends from different denominations to have their Sunday school classes pray for this particular turning point. For that hour during Sunday school I stood with my walker and prayed. I felt closer to God, but nothing more. I do not know whether the classes were praying for me or not — surely someone was! Although I felt no immediate healing and nothing changed physically, I could not reconcile myself to the fact that this drive in me to ask for prayers was for naught. Twelve days later my ankles moved, and my hamstrings showed more strength. That same morning I was able to get into and out of the bathtub by myself for the first time. I was able to balance myself in order to bend for support of the tub. It is for these reasons that I praise the Lord as I ask for more health and healing. In Luke 1:56 (Phillips) we read that Zacharias "beckoned for a writing tablet and wrote the words, 'His name is John.'" Then his power of speech suddenly came back, and his first words were a prayer of thanks to God.

When Jesus prayed for Lazarus He praised God: "Father, I thank Thee that Thou has heard Me." (John 11:41)

The Outreaching Arms of the Cross

Physical healing is not permanent—spiritual healing is. Our bodies are likely to become sick at one time or another and, hopefully, they are made well again. Even so, although we experience complete physical healing, the body will eventually deteriorate with age. In many of His healings Jesus said, "Thy sins are forgiven thee." In such instances, while healing physically, He also proclaimed spiritual healing. Most certainly He demonstrated permanent spiritual healing by His resurrection. The body suffered, the heart ached, and Jesus died physically on the cross. He ascended into heaven, then sent the Holy Spirit at Pentecost to Mary and the disciples (numbering 120 in all), enabling them to pick up their crosses and become witnesses of the Gospel of Jesus Christ. This same Spirit lives on in the hearts and minds of all who accept Jesus Christ as their Lord and Savior.

By His death on the cross and then by the resurrection we are made aware that we must assume the responsibility of our cross. I do believe that we each have a cross. I say a *cross* rather than *crosses*, because I believe that we only need bear one cross. It is our cross of witnessing.

This cross is ours to carry eternally. The outreach of the cross extends in every direction and touches the very core of every experience in life. How we respond to and what we learn from these experiences prepares us to witness for Christ.

This cross is not always easy, because being a Christian is no "apple pie in the sky" life. However, it is the only free and happy life — free because we are no longer burdened with blame, regrets, bitterness, and self-pity. We live a happy life as a result of this freedom. This freedom is no mere happenstance for even the most steadfastly sustained Christian. It is by God's grace and our fellowship with the Holy Spirit that we are able to release our anxieties and are able to be happy when we are responding to trying situations. However, living a life without Christ and assuming a superficial (skin-deep) happiness is a confusing and unrewarding life with no direction and no attainable satisfaction.

Some day we will face physical death, but just as Jesus Christ maintained spiritual life so shall we continue to be spiritually alive as we remain united with Him. "Because I live, you shall live also." If our spirit is joined to the living Christ, we do not need to fear physical death. In fact, we have something beautiful to anticipate. I believe this with all my heart from my own experience with near-death. I believe that after this life we will live fully with Him. Then all the puzzling mysteries of this life will be resolved.

If our cross were as heavy as was that of Jesus Christ, could we carry the load? I would possibly be willing to suffer for my own family—but for the whole world? I cannot comprehend so great a love, yet we know that "God so loved the world that He gave His only-begotten Son, that whosoever believeth in Him should not perish but have everlasting life." (John 3:16)

Faith is not something we are born with or that we simply decide we will obtain. It is God's gift, and He asks us to grow in it through the use of the means of grace. It is something that God asks of us as a prerequisite for receiving physical healing. That kind of faith is believing that He loves us and wants us well. Receiving spiritual healing requires believing, and even more. It requires cooperation on our part, God having given us the strength to do so. "Are there still some among you who hold that 'only believing' is enough? Believing in one God? Well, remember that the devils believe this too—so strongly that they tremble in terror! Dear foolish man! When will you ever learn that 'believing' is useless without *doing* what God wants you to? Faith that does not result in good deeds is not real faith." (James 2:19-20 LB).

As an act of faith, we must submit our *mind,* our *words,* our *thoughts,* and our *actions* to Him. Total submission is essential. Here is where we so easily, and often unconsciously, become trapped—because we are not always willing to surrender completely. Even when we do make this commitment, the task is not easy and we falter constantly. Never a day goes by that we are not tested in every area mentioned. It is encouraging to know that God recognizes and understands our weaknesses and forgives our failures.

"And He said, My Presence shall go with thee" (Exodus 33:14). It is worth understanding that we live in the presence of God, that every expression of our lives is known by His indwelling presence; for it is a gross misapprehension to believe that anything is hidden from Him. Wherever we are, God is! He must constantly suffer the heartbreak and agony of the cross when we continually fail Him and selfishly deny Him.

It is well for us to reflect on each area of our cross of witness. Webster defines *mind* as the element or complex of elements in an individual that feels, perceives, thinks, wills, and especially reasons. Possessing such a combination as this certainly lends intelligence; and intelligence, seasoned with experience and insight, with God prevailing, equates wisdom. Certainly God is the source and power behind our wisdom. To deny this and to pat ourselves on the back for our accomplishments shows a lack of wisdom.

If there is anything in our lives that we should like to change, some habit we should like to break, some crutch of which we should like to rid ourselves, then we must remember that God has given us Christians a renewed free will. This is to say that we have the mind to think and the will to perceive and to decide that there is a snag in our lives. Because we are Spirit-led, because of the influence we have on others—and for our own security in Christ—we must surely want to relinquish what is bothersome or to change the situation. Paul said, "Be transformed by the renewal of your mind." God has also given us reasoning power, and it is only reasonable that God cannot without our co-operation accomplish for us this shedding of old habits and establishment of a new pattern in our lives. We simply cannot say, "When God sees fit, it will happen," and expect our pleas to be granted. Sometimes God's will cannot be accomplished because we continually block the way.

We must, first of all, have an unselfish reason for wanting to abolish our predicament. If we are breaking God's law or the laws of our country, then we have a substantial reason for wanting to abolish this snag. Spiritual laws were established before man. We punish ourselves when we break these laws. "Your job is not to decide whether this law is right or wrong, but to obey it" (James 4:11 LB). There may be many other equally sound reasons. Possibly we have culti-vated a climate that separates us from God, hence making our witness less effective. Whatever the rea-son, we should have a real, unselfish desire to set our house in order; and then we should make a commit-ment to God and to ourselves. It is also helpful to confide in someone else and to have them intercede in prayer for us. The change may come more slowly than we had anticipated.

Keeping in tune with God is not easy, and that charming evil force is pulling hard in the opposite direction. Regardless of appearance, however, evil has never effected any victory if the person be sincere in his desire to be obedient to God. God is the supreme ruler and all victory will be His. To leave the matter up to God with no effort on our part, however, is taking the lazy way out and inviting possible defeat. In other words, we say, "If God doesn't remove this 'speck from my eye,' then it is not wrong or it is not meant to be removed." The devil thrives on such weaknesses. The enjoyment of our vice exceeds the desire to put it behind us.

I have known instances when individuals have sincerely tried to stop some habit in their lives. They have prayed about the situation and others have prayed for them. But because of the time involved, they have become very discouraged. However, with renewed determination, courage, and willpower, they have succeeded and, like all things that are behind us, they have for the most part forgotten the pain suffered while accomplishing their goal. They certainly contend that without God their efforts would have been of no avail. The same applies to illness; we cannot gain or retain our health without trust in God and cooperation with medicine and with divine principles.

One may not be an Albert Einstein or a Jonas Salk, but he can use his God-given mind intelligently. "Are there some wise and understanding men among you? Then your lives will be an example of the humility that is born of true wisdom." (James 3:13 Phillips)

Our choice of *words* has marked influence on other people, for words plant ideas. They also reflect our personalities and constitute one form of witness for Christ. "We all make mistakes in all kinds of ways, but the man who can claim that he never says the wrong thing can consider himself perfect, for if he can control his tongue he can control every other part of his personality!" (James 3:2 Phillips). This is a matter of real consternation to me, for it seems that I constantly spill out and over without taking the time or making the effort to choose the words best suited to express my true feelings. Sometimes I think that if we did not express ourselves at all until we have had time to reflect, better judgment would be used; and what we say would be of more value or far less detrimental. Of course, people sometimes expect appropriate answers *off the cuff*, which puts us at a disadvantage.

In Ephesians 5:4 LB Paul's description is so clear that it needs no further comment: "Dirty stories, foul talk and coarse jokes — these are not for you. Instead, remind each other of God's goodness and be thankful."

Words of profanity bother me. To hear someone put an abusive addendum to his conversation (if it can at all be called a conversation) is not only superfluous but also offensive. This totally unnecessary usage leaves the listener hanging on to the offensive words, while the thought intended by the user of this language is not heard and is often completely lost. Men sometimes seem to think this makes them more masculine. I don't know what appeal it has for women. I have noticed that it has become quite popular with some ladies. If only they could retreat to the hills while spurting some of this obnoxious language and let the echoes return their words, the shock would make them realize how repugnant such coarse, uncouth language is! "Above all things, my brothers, do not use oaths, whether 'by heaven' or 'by earth' or by anything else. When you say yes or no, let it be plain 'Yes' or 'No,' for fear that you expose yourselves to judgment." (James 5:12 NEB)

Charles Allen in his book *The Miracle of Love* mentions a friend who carries a supply of cards to pass out bearing this message:

> The use of PROFANITY is the sublime effort of the ignorant, uncouth, simple-minded, godless man to express himself. "Thou shalt not take the name of the Lord thy God in vain; for the Lord will not hold him guiltless that taketh His name in vain." (Exodus 20:7.)

To blaspheme (intentional indignity against God or sacred things), to deny God is, of course, a very destructive form of profanity. "Believe me, all men's sins can be forgiven and all their blasphemies. But there can never be any forgiveness for blasphemy against the Holy Spirit. That is an eternal sin." (Mark 3:28−29 Phillips)

We are wonderfully created to be God's perfect expression. Affirmative and constructive words can accomplish desired results, helping others acquire spiritual consciousness that can mold their characters. Wholesome words and laughter reflect positive attitudes to life.

Frequently simple, seemingly insignificant words come to us that are important to our progress. I shall never forget one afternoon when I was feeling very low mentally, physically, and spiritually. A friend, our visitation minister's wife, came to sit with me. Casually she broke the silence by telling me how she had spent her early morning hours that day. She stated that she had gone into the garden just at the break of day when everything was quiet and still. She had gathered beans and tomatoes and had listened to the birds as they sang.

She even described a bird perched on the garden post and the pretty tune it carried so early in the morning. Immediately my attitude changed—I yearned inwardly with the desire to become a part once more of the world of which she spoke. I have never been a gardener; but I now realized how much more I missed God's nature and all the little things that we often fail to appreciate than I missed the more complicated luxuries we strive for. Although she was unaware of the impact of the simple words, coming as they did from someone who knows how to appreciate life, this small conversation pulled me from the depths of despair and established a mood for a more affirmative outlook.

WATCHFULNESS

Keep a watch on your words, my brother,
For words are wonderful things;
They are sweet like the bee's fresh honey—
Like the bees they have dangerous stings;
They can bless, like the warm glad sunshine,
And brighten a lonely life;
They can cut in the strife of anger
Like an open two-edged knife.

Let them pass through my lips unchallenged
If their errand is true and kind—
If they come to support the weary,
To comfort and help the blind.
If a bitter revengeful spirit
Prompt the words, let them pass unsaid;
They may flash through a brain like lightening,
Or fall on a heart like lead.

Keep them back, if they're cold and cruel,
Under bar and lock and seal;

The wounds that they make, my brother,
Are always slow to heal.
May peace guard your life, and ever,
From the time of your early youth,
May the words that you daily utter
Be the words of beautiful truth.

— *Author Unknown*

Spending 10 and a half months in a hospital bed and equal time later in convalescing lends ample time for *thoughts,* with hours and days left over. Circumstances cause many people to be idle, unable to stay busy with their hands in order to execute ideas they may have. This has been my own experience. I used to be busy, busy, never getting all the things I dreamed of finished or even started. I hardly had the time for thought, constructive or otherwise. This is good, but of course we are inclined toward the extreme. Now that I am forced to stay at home, I miss being able to do most of these things; but I feel an empathy for others, seeing them so busily occupied both physically and mentally. And since I am forced to observe, I seem to arrive at a better evaluation of the necessary and unnecessary.

Most of the things I had done before my illness involved hands or legs, or both. Everything since has had to be done for me, although I am gradually doing little things for myself. For months, lying in my hospital bed, I studied the formation of clouds drifting over the brick wall, never giving up hope that I would paint them on canvas soon. Recently I have painted my clouds on a couple of pictures by propping the paint brush between my fingers and using my wrist and arms. However, when someone has to open the paints and squeeze the tubes for me, as well as clean my brushes, it would be very easy for me to simply forget the whole thing and brood. At such times, with various disadvantages, one must be cautious. Positive thinking keeps one from losing sanity and directs one to use seemingly adverse situations to advantage. Then gratitude dominates attitude.

I am convinced that the hardest control problem we have to cope with is thought. Thoughts unconsciously (or perhaps consciously) filter into the subconscious, then surface to the conscious, causing us to act or react as we do. Sometimes thoughts, when expressed, are responsible for the actions of others. This is good if we can manage constructive, happy thoughts. It is also true that negative, improper thoughts can be repressed and buried in the subconscious to the point that no guilt at all is felt. Then one becomes as *hard as a rock;* but has not Jesus rolled away the stone from our hearts when He rose from the dead?

I do believe the devil has a larger set of keys for entrance into our thoughts than to any other door we may try to keep locked from him. When we plug one keyhole he tries another — and he never knocks! He is constantly exerting his destructive power in this area. We may get too old, too tired, too content, or too smart for most of his foolishness, but our thoughts are constantly vulnerable.

Like a computer, we constantly feed our thoughts into our subconscious, and the results are just as often fed back to us. Thoughts come in all sizes, shapes, and colors. Jealousy is one form of negative thinking; doubt is another. When bored or tired, we readily think that we are being abused. We are often besieged with anxious, fearful thoughts; we dwell on our misfortunes or on the state of our health. If we check the dictionary for terms such as contention, discord, antagonism, and more, and read the definitions carefully, we may have a mental picture of our negative thoughts.

Sometimes we let tangibles govern our thoughts. We become obsessed with material things. With so many economic demands made of us, earning money certainly seems necessary, and we should think in terms of success in our work; to do less only suppresses our potentials as individuals and limits the power of God. But sometimes worldly aspirations keep us from entrusting ourselves to His care. It is hard to conceive of the idea that just because God provides for "the birds of the air," He will do the same for us.

Although temptations enter our lives, it is our responsibility not to be trapped by negative, emotion-laden thoughts, allowing them to be tossed around in our minds. Emmet Fox in *Find and Use Your Inner Power* says, "Where your attention is, there is your destiny." Entertaining evil thoughts makes one an easy prey to the devil's temptation to actually commit the sin. "He that deviseth to do evil shall be called a mischievous person. The thought of foolishness is sin; and the scorner is an abomination to men." (Proverbs 24:8-9)

Many thoughts of discord and contention are products of neglected communication between two people. The ability to share thoughts is especially essential to a good relationship between husband and wife, but it is certainly a most difficult accomplishment. Expressing our views openly and honestly, and possessing and exercising the capacity to listen with understanding, take a great deal of fortitude, self-control, and empathy.

The mind is seldom free from some form of thinking. It takes mental effort to control thought and emotion. Our problems during most of our lives are believed to be brought about by immaturity. When once—and if ever—we achieve the mature stage, it is said that we cause most of our own problems as a result of our emotions. I feel certain there must be some leeway whereby the existing facts play an influential part. It is important that a person be happy in his work. Beyond that, it is necessary to maintain interest in home, church, friends, hobbies, and especially to have harmonious thoughts concerning God. "You will be judged on whether or not you are doing what Christ wants you to. So watch what you do and what you think." (James 2:12 LB)

While searching the Scriptures for revelations on thought, I was enlightened by the number of verses in both Old and New Testaments where *thought* and *heart* were used together, manifesting that where the *thought* is there is the heart—that the *heart* is not just a physical organ but a spiritual power.

> And Jesus knowing their thoughts said, wherefore think ye evil in your hearts? (Matthew 9:4)
>
> But when Jesus perceived their thoughts, He answering said unto them, What reason ye in your hearts? (Luke 5:22)

And Jesus perceiving the thought of their hearts, took a child, and set him by Him. (Luke 9:47)

Search me, O God, and know my heart; try me and know my thoughts. (Psalms 139:23)

The admonition: "Be doers of the Word, and not hearers only," does not necessarily imply only physical *actions* or deeds. It can mean utilization of our intelligence, using faith, and putting convictions into practice. "If faith does not lead to action, it becomes a lifeless thing" (James 2:17 NEB). Again, works are not always outward actions. Works can be our mental thought, discipline and self-control, meditation time, prayers for others, witnessing by being Christlike even though unable to witness publicly, taking care of one's health and one's appearance, and exhibiting fortitude even when bored and lonely.

"So be careful how you act . . . make the most of every opportunity you have for doing good. Don't act thoughtlessly, but try to find out and do whatever the Lord wants you to do" (Ephesians 5:15-17 LB). "For by grace are ye saved through faith; and that not of yourselves. It is the gift of God; not of works, lest any man should boast" (Ephesians 2:8-9). While it is true that one is not saved by piling up good works, most of us possess energy, talents, and time that can be utilized for the Lord's work. There are multiple needs to be fulfilled, and much good that one can and should do. There are never enough people willing to teach Sunday schools or to fill many other places of service in our churches. There never comes a time in our lives when we are not obligated to God to do our part in carrying on His work here on earth. "We are God's handiwork, created in Christ Jesus to devote ourselves to the good deeds for which God has designed us." (Ephesians 2:10 NEB).

I could not begin to list the numerous acts of human kindness rendered me during these months of illness. There were many who stayed by my bedside to relieve my family for a few hours from strain and tension — while concealing their own tenseness. Many prepared food for my family, books and flowers were brought to me, and one neighbor's boys mowed our lawn. Even now friends take time out from their busy schedules to take me places where I need to go. Most of all, their visits cheer me. One friend even shops weekly for my groceries. This is not a drop in the bucket compared to the total favors that have been done for me.

RESULTS

God proffered me a simple task,
Though why so small I dared not ask.
I took it and blessed it;
   I loved it all the while;
I warmed it with gladness
   and a great big smile.
Right away the lowly duty
Took on dignity and beauty,
And sooner than perhaps you'd guess
My task grew big with happiness.
             — *Elizabeth Landewear*

Sometimes we are afraid to assume the responsibility of witnessing and telling someone about Christ because we do not have all the answers. We are afraid of leaving them disillusioned or frustrated. We have often said or heard someone else remark, "Who am

I to say!" But we should not hesitate to *plant the seed.* When one is searching for answers he cannot expect all the answers from one source; he needs to search further. We should not feel that we have failed when we are not able to supply all the answers. If we have planted a seed, it will very likely germinate and grow— whether the seed be planted by word of mouth as a result of our mind and thoughts, which are dedicated to Christ, or if it be planted by our own actions. We may even say, "My very actions are not a good example!" We all "fall short of the glory of God," and so we can learn and let others learn by our mistakes. We can continue to improve and to witness for Christ as we grow. When Peter helped the man at the temple entrance he said, "What I have, I give you." (Acts 3:6 NEB)

"Christ hath redeemed us from the curse of the Law, being made a curse for us . . . that we might receive the promise of the Spirit through faith." (Galatians 3:13-14)

Christ not only died on the cross for our sins but also has gone to prepare a place for us. He sits at the right hand of God the Father in order to intercede for us and enable us to be in communion with the Holy Spirit. How busy He must be! Because of the physical limitations of the people through whom He works He could not reach the entire population of this world. But He promised: "I will pray the Father, and He shall give you another comforter, that He may abide with you forever." (John 14:16)

The cross on which Christ died to save us is to me symbolic of the fact that we should *cross* out all devious, uncontrolled words, thoughts, and actions that may hinder us in receiving this gift of God. Christ should be invited into our lives so that our *minds* may be used to think His *thoughts* and so that our *words* and *actions* may express His love.

The resurrection of our Lord gives me the assurance that no soul, regardless of how calloused, how buried in sin, has become so hard that Christ cannot *roll away the stone.* Then the Holy Spirit may enter and all things will become less complicated. Life can be fuller and happier. Our "cross of witnessing" becomes positive and alive.

10

My Lifesaving Mechanical Friend

Like a round-table, the days rotated into weeks and the weeks into months; and like a round-table, it seemed we were right back where we started. I dared not give thought to how long I was to be confined to the hospital room, nor anticipate going home. I accepted, though never quite adapted to, the confinement. Daily living with the hospital schedule was unmitigated routine now. Dana had read the records of a few cases of the Guillain-Barre syndrome to me. Every case had completely recovered after from a few weeks to three months. I was positive that a three-month duration would be all (and quite likely more) than I could possibly tolerate. However, after three, four, and five months I conceded that I had set a record.

I had setbacks such as flu and colds. Because of a precarious lung condition, extreme caution was necessary, and flu and colds were not considered minor by any means. Immediately upon entering the hospital I contracted pneumonia. This was caused by the paralysis and was soon cured. From the very beginning of illness, allergies flared up and were a constant and exasperating problem. My entire body was covered with rashes and welts most of the time. As a result, I suffered tremendous pain and itching. I was allergic to absolutely everything, including medication for the allergy. Flowers had to be removed from my room. Perfumes and other scents within nose range were and continue to be a source of irritation. My eyes, nose, and mouth poured excessively because of allergies; and because of the necessary constant suctioning, there was heavy bleeding. Both nose and mouth were extremely sensitive and painful because of constant irritation. Those were devastatingly horrible days — unreal in every sense. I was told that I should exercise every muscle that would move as often as possible. By late evenings tension had usually taken hold of me and my nerves felt shattered. Also, this was the time of day that I felt fatigue the most. I found that a good remedy for these trying times was to throw myself into exercise. About all I could do was to twist my shoulders and back, but I found that it did help to release those pangs of tension.

There were times when the tube in my throat had to be changed. These occasions were dreaded by everyone involved, including the doctor, I'm sure, for they knew how painful this procedure was. I always tried to persuade him to put it off as long as possible. This was such an agonizing process that I could not restrain tears. The endotracheal tube is made of plastic and is about 6 inches long and three-quarter of an inch in diameter, with an elbow-type angle in the middle. Not having seen this contraption but judging from the feeling of wearing it, I had in my own mind described this tube as a *metal* windpipe, 8 inches long and 2 inches wide. Anyway, the entire tube was inserted into the opening in the throat (made when the tracheotomy was performed) and was extended into the lungs. As described previously, suctioning to remove secretions from the lungs was made possible through this artificial trachea by extending a long spaghetti-like plastic hose into the opening in the trachea and then into the lungs. The other end of the plastic hose was attached to a suctioning machine. The tube was also connected to the respirator, which breathed for me. Because of the danger of infection, the tube was removed and a new one installed about once every month or two. The doctor accomplished this by pulling it out with force because the flesh would grow around and over it in places. Since I could not breathe without the respirator, there was no time to dally; another "trachea" had to be forced into place immediately. With the mission accomplished, the doctor feigned complacency as he left the room without looking back. Obviously he was almost as bothered as I was. He always returned later to see if he were forgiven.

I shall never forget the last "trachea" that was removed—without the need for a replacement. After 287 days on the breathing machine, that was indeed a day for celebration! For a long time I had practiced breathing without the respirator. A little red light blinked when I *triggered* this machine (took a breath on my own). In the beginning I could barely trigger it once, and this required intense concentration. The lung muscles were very weak from having been paralyzed for such a long period, but I had also forgotten how to breathe. The therapist had to teach me how to inhale and exhale, how to pull the abdomen in and let it out. It was as new to me as if I had never known how to breathe. After one breath, then two, and so on for weeks I eventually was able to be taken off the respirator a few minutes at a time. Eventually I was off for an hour and more until finally my waking hours were off the machine completely and I was actually breathing of my own effort. As I write about this, sitting here breathing normally again, it strikes me as incredible — absolutely unbelievable — that man has invented a machine so intricate as to actually supply life-sustaining breath for a human being for almost a year. With due credit to the excellent care I received, there were never any extreme complications, such as pneumonia, from this machine. This reality makes me ashamed when I forget to praise God, when I let insignificant things enter my life and for one moment forget to be grateful.

Naturally there came the time for sleeping without the respirator — a device on which I had learned to depend. It had taken me months to trust this piece of equipment enough to go to sleep. Now I had to wean myself from it; but I was not afraid. I resented anyone's suggestion that if it were not for fear I could simply start breathing and forget my respirator. I found this belief to be true for some, even those who had been exposed to illnesses but who were without personal conflict. Even now there are some misunderstanding souls who, not knowing the necessity of muscle return and strength, think that I could walk without any support if it were not for fear. This, of course, is a misconception, because I have no desire to let my progress be hampered by fear. There was, and is, little left of which to be afraid. If I had not learned trust in God by this time, then the night spent on the floor had been an agonizing and deceptive mirage.

I am grateful that my doctor and therapist never exhibited such an attitude. In fact, the confidence that most people, including the nurses, had in me throughout my illness was a consolation which stimulated a desire to do my best in all endeavors. They never tried to force me into any new developments. Consequently I was able to sense the time for drifting off to sleep and trusting in God to let me breathe. I can't explain it—it just happened, and everyone felt relief that another great step had been made. I make these statements concerning the attitudes of others toward me although I realize that this may not be applicable to everyone recuperating from some tragedy, illness, or other circumstance.

After so much rambling let's go back to the momentous day when the "trachea" was removed and the respirator was rolled out of the room. I was crowned *Queen of the Ohio* (the manufacturers' name for the respirator) by the inhalation therapist, complete with crown and picture-taking as the *Ohio* was wheeled into the hall. Two-hundred-eighty-seven days of waiting, hoping, and praying by literally hundreds of people for this noteworthy day, and it had finally come! Unbelievable!

My mechanical friend had a companion. I was

given bronchial treatments several times a day with a smaller and less complicated machine.

A few months after entering the hospital a neighbor patient was celebrating her birthday in the room across the hall. I was told that it was customary for the hospital kitchen to bake and present the patients with a decorated cake on such an occasion. I thought this was nice, but my birthday was not until February 22. Thus I was sure they wouldn't have to plan a cake for me. I would be celebrating my birthday at home, or who knows where! This was wishful thinking on my part, for I literally spent every holiday of the year in Room 553. These included my wedding anniversary in November, Hallowe'en, Thanksgiving, Christmas, my birthday, every state and national holiday, also a hurricane and Groundhog Day.

I was remembered on every occasion. Ted decorated a beautiful tree in my room for Christmas and packages were stacked high. Our family, including the grandbaby Kyle, spent Christmas Eve together and opened our packages in my room. The fifth floor personnel gave me a beautiful yellow gown and robe. I was indeed pleased that they had included me in their Christmas celebration. I actually helped plan the family's Christmas dinner from my bed. My vocal cords were still paralyzed and so I was not talking; but almost everyone had learned to lip-read after my lips began to function enough to form words.

My birthday was another elaborate occasion. There wasn't sufficient room to display all the cards. And there was the special birthday cake, followed by a parade of hospital staff singing "Happy Birthday."

It was the middle of March when I was taken off the breathing respirator permanently and was allowed to be rolled outside. By that time I was also able to sit in a wheelchair. It had been almost one year since I had sensed the smell and feeling of fresh air, wind, and sunshine, and equally that long since I had seen grass, a tree, a car, a house, or the outside of a building, a pavement, a bird. The hospital grounds were lovely, with azaleas and crepe myrtle in full bloom. I could only express my emotions with tears for this unbelievable reality, and certainly with gratitude that so long and hard a battle was nearly won by God's unfailing grace and the efforts and compassion of many doctors, hospital staff, family, and friends. I certainly sensed what God must have felt when He looked at His handiwork and "saw that it was good." I have been told many times that my attitude and determination helped to bring me through a great deal; but without God and this rooting section even a fair attitude would have been impossible to maintain.

April Fool's Day rolled around. That was the day set for me to go home—not because it was April Fool's Day but just as a coincidence. Going home took quite a lot of preparation because all kinds of equipment had to be set up at home. Maid service and 24-hour nursing also had to be secured. One friend spent days at the telephone trying to find exactly the right person to fit my needs for home care.

Two days before check-out day I contracted a cold as well as having acquired a sunburn from the short time spent outside the day before. Because of these ailments, the doctor warned me not to let my hopes for

111

going home get too high. I refused to be anything less than optimistic. But when he made his rounds on Saturday morning, my lungs were not clear enough for his approval. He declared another week of bed rest — in the hospital. After another week I could go home, provided my lungs were free of congestion.

Through that day I maintained a fairly nonchalant attitude. However, when it was about time for Dan to go home, I was feeling totally defeated, and poor Dan, as usual, caught the brunt of my turmoil. No one could seem to understand why after 10 and a half months one more week would be of any significance. Of course, they were right; but for a few hours I didn't see it that way, and I wasn't very reasonable. Sensing real anxiety and pity for myself, I became petulant as I pictured myself being wheeled into my house rather than walking in as in the days of old. I went so far as to complain that since I would have to go home as an invalid in a wheelchair I had just as soon stay in the hospital. I did not sincerely mean this, of course.

By morning I was no longer feeling sorry for myself, and the inhalation therapist went to work to rid me of the congestion on my lungs. By use of proper equipment, and with their practically standing me on my head four times a day and beating me on the back to make me cough, I was in acceptable shape the following week. This time I made no plans until the doctor gave his positive announcement. This confirmed, the packing crew consisting of Ted, nurses, aides, and the therapist went to work. Having practically established a permanent residence in this room, it took half a day to gather my belongings, as can well be imagined. Upon completing this chore, as many as could avail themselves followed me to the hospital exit.

Saying goodbye to a hospital staff seems simple enough and certainly of little significance. But we were all choked with mixed emotions. There were sad goodbyes; yet there was a glad thrill that such a memoriable day, so long anticipated, had finally come to pass. I shall forever be grateful to these fantastic people.

The arrival at home, with friends waiting for me, was also full of emotion. Everything looked great — even the weeds in my flower beds expressed life. Someday I'll be working those beds again! The children next door had put a "Welcome Home" sign in my yard. Entering through the back door, I was thrilled to see familiar surroundings. My own furniture, paintings, bric-a-brac *et cetera* made me tremble with emotion.

Even our little dog Butch, a terrier, greeted me, shaking with excitement. He had become very despondent when I was in the hospital and had actually moped to the point that he was ill.

I was still very weak and tired, but after getting settled at home, I began to improve rapidly. Ted was at home all summer and, as usual, managed everything like a real pro. By fall, when he returned to school, I was able to manage the household from my bed or wheelchair.

And thus began my outpatient recovery.

11

The Five Senses

This week, almost 14 months after leaving the hospital, I am realizing prodigious strides in the form of independence. This may seem of no consequence to you who have never faced the reality of constant, round-the-clock care — of having the very simplest of things done for you, of being unable to do the things that even a crawling baby can do.

For more than two years now I have had someone with me constantly, day and night. This has involved dressing and undressing me, preparing the food for me and for a long time feeding me as well; also brushing my teeth, lifting me from lying to sitting to standing positions, and vice versa. After I was able to be propped up in bed and could read, the book or magazine pages had to be turned for me. I couldn't talk then, but I adopted a little click that got attention. I still unconsciously find myself using that click now and then. In fact, I used this noise so long and so often then to get attention that many times after being able to talk I have actually awakened myself from a deep sleep with this click-click noise.

I still cannot pick up the pages of a book or the likes, but gradually I have become able to push the pages back with my fingers. This recapitulation of activities that necessarily had to be done for my daily function could go on and on.

Help has come and gone. Some situations have been pleasant, some not so pleasant. Life these past two years has been full of rare and sometimes complex experiences. There have also been many rewarding times. I have acquired much knowledge about and patience with all sorts of personalities. I have certainly benefited from being afforded the opportunity of living at home and surrounded by these people. As I reflect, I recall that there have even been moments of humor on occasion.

I am about to enjoy more privacy and independence, as I mentioned in the first sentence of this chapter. I am now able to stay alone, and there is no need to say that I am elated and overcome with pride and happiness in this new adventure of doing things for myself.

I still cannot do the necessary heavy housework (many women will envy me), but I can prepare food with some limitations. I had limitations with cooking and housework before this handicap existed—such limitations as boredom and the feeling of abuse. I was without a doubt being alienated from more refined and resourceful stations in society. Now I thrill at being able to open a can. When I hear women complain of being tired or bored with routine housework, I secretly envy this type of fatigue.

With my walker nearby, I lean against the kitchen

cabinets and I can do almost anything I like in my kitchen. With a backward prop and a certain twist I can get in and out of the refrigerator for food. Soon I will need to manipulate standing on the scales. In the kitchen, care is taken to place things within certain bounds so that I don't have to reach too far or too high, or stoop too low. Caps on jars and bottles are left slightly loose, since I have little strength in and practically no grasp with my hands. I can manage the movement of dishes and cooking utensils from the table to the kitchen sink by simply sliding them across the cabinets. I can even load and unload the dishwasher. Unloading is a sinuous task in case you're getting bored with all this emphasis on household drudgery. It actually takes brain power.

With my bath the tactics used are not the usual, to say the least. For instance, there is no such thing as stepping in and out of the tub or shower. I have refused from the beginning to have bars and such built in because I have been sure that step-by-step I would progress until I would not have the need for these extras. To get into the tub, I brace myself to a sitting position on the commode and then I scoot to the side of the tub. I lift one leg at a time up and into the tub. This I have to do with my arms because I cannot lift my legs under their own power. Then I simply slide down the side of the tub. All this is done before I run the water, of course. I am able to lift myself out of the tub onto the side, and from then on it is the reverse of getting in. It is a big improvement from those days, not too far in the past, when any form of transportation for me was accomplished by means of a hydraulic lift.

Because of therapy, and the fact that they conceal my leg braces, my wearing apparel consists almost entirely of slacks and easy-to-button blouses. I have my own method of dressing too. Zippers are out, but after several attempts per button, I can pull a button through a buttonhole. It's a real catastrophe though to have a button slide out right before your eyes, and just when you are sure it is intact. Did someone say, "Praise the Lord, anyway"?

Last but not least are the rather newly acquired leg braces. It takes me 20 minutes of pulling and tugging with all those buckles, straps, and strings. But the important thing is that I can do it, and it is excellent exercise for the stomach. I sleep in still another set of braces, less complicated than my daytime pair. These braces are worn in order to keep the ligaments from stretching and to keep my feet from dropping.

With regard to these braces, I am reminded of a dream I had a few nights after getting them. Immediately after I started wearing them I began to notice women's pretty shoes. One night I dreamed that a friend had taken me shopping for a pair of shoes. I wanted the prettiest pair possible; so this took a long time. Finally we found a beautiful pair, as dainty as Cinderella's! I was so thrilled with them! On our way home we passed a deep, dark well. We stopped and I put my shoes on a ledge that was around the well. I'm sure I do not need to tell the rest of the story. Yes, one shoe fell down that deep dark well — gone forever, and I was crushed.

Putting on makeup is another newly acquired distinction. In the past, someone had to do that for me on the special occasions when I wore any.

Since I have written chapter 8 telling about the aid that was required to get my tubes of paint open, I have learned how, as well as gained additional strength to open them by twisting the caps with pliers from the tool chest.

My, how much we take for granted! Going 9 months without talking seems absolutely unreal, even to me now that I can manage almost any word. I received speech therapy after I was out of the hospital. This therapy was very beneficial, but dormant muscles had to return and weak muscles had to gain strength before there was a noticeable difference in my speech. How well I remember the very first attempt at trying to talk! No one, including myself, knew what to expect. I did not even remember how to talk, nor could I think of anything to say. That part of my brain had been dormant for a long, long time. With the first try nothing happened. There was not a sound. After so long, would I ever talk again? Then in two weeks they deflated the balloon inside the trachea again, and this time, to our delight, a weird, gruff squawk came from some-where way down there. I had never heard that voice before! But the noise was sufficient to let us know that quality would come later.

I was still not off the respirator long enough to do much talking. The balloons I described had to be deflated in order for me to talk, and then inflated again when I had finished. One morning I decided to call three friends. Two of these ladies were curious enough to question me until they recognized my voice. The third, however, was already late for an appointment elsewhere and she did not have time for any crackpot telephone calls, and she hung up on me. That's just exactly how distorted my voice was at that time.

I have suffered a few falls since I have been home. These were each due to exhaustion, pushing just a little too much. Hopefully I am learning when enough is enough.

The physical and emotional strain of making an appearance in public or of being in crowds was, until very recently, overwhelming. I would shed tears very easily, partly from weakness and partly from gratitude.

Then a few weeks ago, while taking my usual practice hike down the long corridor during one of my therapy sessions, I suddenly decided to give it (walking) a try. I turned loose my hold from the two who were walking along side of me for support and took off on my own. Now, that is exaggerated slightly. The taking off was actually scooting, because I still cannot pick my feet up without braces. Neither can I stop completely, because I do not have strong enough muscle return at this time for balance. However, it was the nearest thing to walking that I had experienced for many a month, and the excitement ran high all over the place. Everyone lined up to watch me perform. My blood tingled with excitement. I felt like I had just gotten off a merry-go-round. The telephone lines were kept busy that evening and I was too excited to sleep very well that night. That was additional assurance — *physical* assurance — that I would walk again. It was just a few weeks before that the Sunday school classes had prayed for this very thing to happen. There were also many others who were continually praying for this. This is such a tremendous improvement from the time that I was strapped to the tilt table. How I ached, in the early months on that hospital bed, to be able to be in an upright position! Finally I forgot what it was like. Then when I was finally (after 13 months) strapped and slowly rolled upward, there was some disappointment because I had so little sensation. Yet mentally I reminded myself of how long it had been, and I was pleased.

I am reminded of the day they did the brain scan. There was a lot of nervous anxiety. Was there a brain tumor? During those many months there was no way of knowing whether or not there was brain damage. Even in the intensive care unit I was aware that some sort of brain damage was suspected (or expected). I knew that my mind seemed perfectly sound and normal so far as I could tell. I heard and knew everything and I had not lost my reasoning — except perhaps those times when the pain and hallucinations were nearly unbearable. Of course, no one else could know that, for without talking or moving I had no way of responding. But even I wondered what could possibly follow. I was frightened at the thought of mental incapacitation. I did not know that even my speech had to return before it could be said there was no damage to the brain — and that was 9 long months returning. So, one must surely understand why I am so ecstatic with having the ability to think, the ability to use what creative talents I may have, and why I am so grateful for life.

I think of the beautifully adjusted people who cannot see nor hear, especially when I read the works of

Helen Keller. These people have made the very best of life regardless of their handicaps. It is then that I am reminded of the time when

> I could not *see,*
>> and then I saw yellow polka dots;
>
> I could not *hear,*
>> and I could not see to lip read;
>
> I could not *taste,* nor could I *eat,*
>> and I was hungry;
>
> I could not *smell,*
>> I don't know why;
>
> I could not *touch,*
>> I WAS PARALYZED.

12

Sifted Gold

For my own satisfaction I have been compelled to seek the truth concerning whether or not we are *tried* or *tested.* If so, by what force are we tested? Is it by God or the devil? Are our sufferings sometimes brought about to test the faith of others?

After Dan's extended illnesses I was certain that we had now encountered our *trials* and *tribulations.* I felt comfortable in the erroneous assumption that we had been sufficiently *tried* and *tested.* Surely our faith must have been proved, conditioned by the fact that Dan had endured and had survived, and had become conditioned to the status of his health. He had overcome the worries involved for the one who is the head of the household — and about my ability to sustain the load that the mate cannot avoid. Now with my own illness, we are each having to respond to the same situation in reverse order. I see in Dan now the same agony of releasing the pressures that I suffered with his heart attack. For years after his coronary I was scared when he was out of my sight. It was so hard to put him on his own again. Yet it is so important, because we do not want to remain helpless forever. When I was so very ill and was trying to rationalize, I cried just as David did in Psalms 66:10, "For Thou, O God, hast proved us; Thou hast tried us, as silver is tried."

I have since decided that we are sometimes tried again and again, not only in the realm of physical illnessess but, for some of us, in every conceivable way. I had responded to Dan's illness and the problems thereafter to the best of my ability, and certainly I grew from the experience. However, as the years passed I had become busy again doing Christian work. Mostly, but not always, it was to glorify God's name. One ingenious method the devil uses is to entice us into Christian works that we may further our own repute or foster our own ambitions.

While writing this book I have put more concentrated effort than ever before into the reading of God's Word. This probing has been to satisfy my own soul's searching desire as well as to find answers to questions asked by others concerning my attitude toward this illness. Thereby I am convinced that when we endeavor to become more knowledgeable concerning God's purpose and will for our lives, *temptations* or *testings* from every direction tend to block our vision and our pursuit of wisdom and fortitude.

I believe these demoralizing temptations are of the devil. "The devil shall cast some of you into prison, that ye may be tried" (Revelation 2:10). We must not allow evil to cause our purpose to be defeated. It is the result of our response to temptations and to testings that determines our success in overcoming and measuring up to our full potentials. Although we may not achieve immediate success, we do, if victorious over temptation, revere God's name and make ourselves accessible for His use. "Blessed is the man that endureth temptation; for when he is tried, he shall receive the crown of life, which the Lord hath promised to them that love Him" (James 1:12). I find hope and consolation when I read and reflect on the order in which the following is written: "Many shall be purified, and made white, and tried." (Daniel 12:10)

I do not believe that God brings illnesses or obstacles of any kind into our lives in order to test us for evil. "No one under trial or temptations should say, 'I am being tempted by God'; for God is untouched by evil, and does not Himself tempt anyone" (James 1:13 NEB). He allows trials to come—trials which quite often man brings on himself with his sins.

God knows all; but we do not know the strength of our own faith until we have been tried. It is much like seeing a child eat too much candy. We can tell him he is going to have a stomachache. But not until he has experienced the actual pain can he relate the eating of too much candy to a stomachache. We are often opinionated as to the way others handle a particular matter; but we cannot truly have insight into their problems until or unless we have experienced a similar situation. Even then we do not have their natures or know their hearts. Since we so often have no conception of our own faith, it is for our own growth and salvation that we are allowed testings. Amid trials we obtain "the salvation which is even now in readiness and will be revealed at the end of time." (1 Peter 1:5 NEB)

Are our sufferings brought about to test the faith

of others? It seems valid that our sufferings can be used to test the faith of others just the same as they can be used to test our own faith. If it is the faith and prayers of others that sometimes bring about our healings, then surely our sufferings can be used to test the faith of others. When someone near and dear to us is suffering, whether from illness or something else, we certainly suffer vicariously with them. If it be a member of the family, we go through all the hardships involved. When we experience this intensity of sharing, then surely our faith is subjected to trials.

The following questions have presented themselves many times: Is it necessary that we all be tried? If so, in every sphere of life? Why are some (usually the good) constantly put to the test while others get off scot-free? The Bible says, "The Lord trieth the righteous." (Psalm 11:5)

I found answers to such questions that satisfied me in 1 Peter 1:6-7 NEB: "This is cause for great joy, even though now you smart for a little while, *if need be,* under trials of many kinds. Even gold passes through the assayer's fire, and more precious than perishable gold is faith which has stood the test." I was disappointed to discover that some translations of this Scripture have failed to include these words in their interpretations: *"if need be."* Who but God can be the arbitrator of these three simple words? Certainly it is not you or I.

In Paul's Letter to the Thessalonians, when he says, "God, which trieth our hearts," refers to the broken hearts when the Word of God was not accepted but was "shamefully mistreated at Philippi." We have those with us today whose hearts are *tried* when their witness for Christ is not honored.

Even God's Word is *tried* today as in the days of King David (2 Samuel 22:34). Psalms 18:30 says, "The Word of the Lord is tried."

If I were to cite any particular facet or area in my life for which I believe I have been (and continue to be) *tested* or *tried* the most during my illness, other than faith, I suppose it would be patience. I was told in the early stages that the disease would not tolerate impatience, and it is certainly true. By exercising patience (through consciousness of the need, nevertheless faltering many times) I am learning to accept the slow return to health and normalcy, also to accept my incapabilities for the moment while maintaining emotional stability. I am learning to receive as well as to give. I am trying to maintain pride and self-esteem with discretion and reasonability. It is difficult to have our pride drained from us in every conceivable way, and I'm convinced that it is necessary to pull through all unpleasant situations with some pride. Hopefully I am learning to tolerate the constant training and changing of necessary domestic help. I acknowledge the patience that others have shown and continue to show me. "Forgetting those things which are behind and reaching forth unto those things which are before, I press toward the mark." (Philippians 3:13)

But He Knoweth the way that I take;
When He hath tried me, I shall come forth as gold.
(Job 23:10)